AMERICAN**POP**ICONS

Guggenheim Hermitage MUSEUM

Published on the occasion of the exhibition
American Pop Icons
Guggenheim Hermitage Museum, Las Vegas
May 15–November 2, 2003
Organized by Susan Davidson

Entries by Rachel Haidu are reprinted with permission from
From Pop to Now: Selections from the Sonnabend Collection
(The Frances Young Tang Teaching Museum and Art Gallery at
Skidmore College, 2002).

Entries by Jennifer Blessing and Nancy Spector are reprinted
from *Guggenheim Museum Collection: A to Z* (Guggenheim
Museum, 2001); Artist's Biographies (except Tom Wesselmann)
are reprinted from *Rendezvous: Masterpieces from the Centre
Georges Pompidou and the Guggenheim Museums* (Guggenheim
Museum, 1998).

ISBN 0-89207-296-2 (hardcover)
ISBN 0-89207-296-0 (softcover)

Guggenheim Museum Publications
1071 Fifth Avenue
New York, New York 10128

Guggenheim Hermitage Museum
3355 Las Vegas Boulevard South
Las Vegas, Nevada 89109
www.guggenheimlasvegas.org

Design: Cassey L. Chou, with Marcia Fardella and
Christine Sullivan
Production: Tracy L. Hennige
Editorial: Meghan Dailey, Laura Morris

Printed in Germany by Cantz

Front cover (detail) and back cover:
Roy Lichtenstein, *Preparedness*, 1968 (plate 16)

Contents

The Solomon R. Guggenheim Foundation

Director's Statement

American Pop Icons is the third exhibition to be presented in Las Vegas at the Guggenheim Hermitage Museum as part of an ongoing collaboration between two of the world's leading cultural institutions. Drawing from and expanding on the rich holdings of diverse collections with the aim of making them accessible to a wider audience, the Guggenheim Hermitage Museum continues to organize significant exhibitions, promoting scholarly research that extends the scope of public awareness through its presentations and publications.

Inaugurated in 2001, the "jewel-box" exhibition space within the Venetian Resort-Hotel-Casino was designed by internationally recognized architect Rem Koolhaas and has proven to be a unique and versatile contemporary space in which to showcase artworks from very different time periods. Following two exhibitions of European masterpieces ranging from the Renaissance and Baroque periods to the early twentieth century from the collections of the Solomon R. Guggenheim Museum, New York, the Hermitage State Museum, St. Petersburg, and the Kunsthistorisches, Vienna, the Guggenheim Hermitage Museum now presents an exhibition of paintings and sculpture by American Pop artists, expanding on the strong collection of the Solomon R. Guggenheim Museum.

American Pop Icons includes seminal works by some of the twentieth century's most celebrated artists. From Robert Rauschenberg's Combine paintings to Jasper Johns's *Flags*, and from Andy Warhol's *Campbell's Soup Cans* to Roy Lichtenstein's oversized comic-strip inspired canvases, the works shown here represent a key moment in American art history in which artists turned away from the painterly concerns of Abstract Expressionism toward an engagement with the culture that surrounded them. Internationally, the focus of the art world at this time was very much on America. In many ways, the artists' works reflect this, revealing the nature of art-making in an all-encompassing consumer culture of the time.

Thomas Krens
Director, The Solomon R. Guggenheim Foundation

Preface and Acknowledgments

Numerous individuals and institutions have offered their assistance to the creation of this exhibition. On behalf of the Solomon R. Guggenheim Foundation and the Guggenheim Hermitage Museum, I would like to extend our deepest gratitude to the lenders. Their participation is critical to the success of any exhibition and made even more difficult when the artworks involved are so iconic to the history of twentieth-century art. Ileana Sonnabend and Antonio Homem of the Sonnabend Collection enthusiastically embraced the concept for this exhibition from its inception and their loans serve as a cornerstone of this exhibition. Artists Jasper Johns and James Rosenquist have each supported the exhibition with loans of their artwork from their private collections; their individual engagement is a credit to their ongoing interest in the history of Pop art. Jose Berardo, Bernard Jacobson, Torsten Lilja, and several anonymous lenders have each allowed key artworks from their collection to join the fabric of the exhibition.

For assistance in obtaining loans, I have relied on the considerable knowledge and good will of a select group of colleagues in the trade: Paul Gray of the Richard Gray Gallery, Chicago and New York; James Mayor of the Mayor Gallery, London; Bob Monk; Edward Nahem of Edward Nahem Fine Art, New York; and Jennifer Vorbach of C & M Arts, New York. Each has offered their trust and cooperation for which I am most grateful. Additional assistance in securing important loans has been capably provided by Isabel Soares Alves, Laura Bloom, Ann Carley, Beverly Coe, Michael Harrigan, Robert Hollister, Lynn Kearcher, Josey Kraft, Esty Neuman, Xan Price, Sarah Taggart, and Christine Zehner.

Sylvia Sleigh, Lawrence Alloway's widow and herself a renowned portrait painter, and her archivist, Hephsie Loeb, graciously opened the Lawrence Alloway archive for my review. Access to important archival documentation from the *Six Painters and the Object* exhibition has been provided by Lynn Underwood, Director of Information Integration and Management at the Guggenheim. At the Menil Collection, Houston, my former colleagues, Geraldine Aramanda, Archivist; Phil Heagy, Librarian; and Mary Kadish, Assistant Registrar, fielded numerous research queries. Walter Hopps first informed my understanding of Pop art, while Don Quaintance, Julia Blaut, and Simonetta Fraquelli each in their own way continue to extend my research. Woodfin Camp, who represents photographer Ken Heyman, readily made available photographs of the period while Kim Bush, Photography and Permissions Manager at the Guggenheim, provided images of the artworks in the Guggenheim's collection.

My curatorial colleagues at the Guggenheim— Sarah Bancroft, Tracey Bashkoff, Jennifer Blessing, Nancy Spector, Kara Vander Weg, and Joan Young—have contributed insightful entries on the artworks in the exhibition. I am most appreciative of their dedication and camaraderie in producing this material in such a timely manner. Charles Stainback, Director of the Frances Young Tang Teaching Museum and Art Gallery generously agreed to allow texts written by Rachal Haidu for his recent touring exhibition *From Pop to Now: Selections from the Sonnabend Collection* to be reprinted here.

The spirited engagement of the entire staff at the Guggenheim Museum has assured the successful realization of this exhibition. Thomas Krens, Director; Lisa Dennison,

Deputy Director and Chief Curator; Marc Steglitz, Deputy Director for Finance and Operations; and Anthony Calnek, Deputy Director for Communications and Publishing have guided every aspect of this exhibition and I am most grateful for their support and continued encouragement. The gifted and dedicated staff of art professionals at the museum have greatly contributed to a smooth undertaking of this project. In particular, I would like to thank Laurel MacMillan, Hilla Rebay International Intern, and Aaron Moulton, Intern, for their research and administrative support throughout all stages of planning this exhibition. Karen Meyerhoff, Managing Director for Collections, Exhibitions, and Design, and Marion Kahan, Exhibition Program Manager have swiftly guided the planning aspects of this project. Meryl Cohen, Director of Registration and Art Services; Ted Mann, Assistant Registrar for Collections and Outgoing Loans; and MaryLouise Napier, Registrar for Collection Exhibitions, deftly executed the complex shipping arrangements. Ana Luisa Leite, Manager of Exhibition Design, and Dan Zuzunaga, Exhibition Design Assistant, contributed significantly to the design of the exhibition. Julie Barten, Conservator, Exhibitions and Administration; Eleanora Nagy, Sculpture Conservator; and Carol Stringari, Senior Conservator of Contemporary Art, worked closely with me on the care and protection of all the works in the exhibition. Scott Wixon, Manager of Art Services and Preparations; David Bufano, Chief Preparator; and Jeffrey Clemens, Associate Preparator, in New York prepared the artworks for shipping, while Eric Edler, Director of Art Services, Guggenheim Hermitage Museum, and Max Fernando Bensuaski, Project Manager,

in Las Vegas seamlessly moved and installed them and Mary Ann Hoag, Lighting Designer, has carefully lit them. Numerous other individuals in various departments throughout the museum have offered their expertise. In particular, I would like to thank in New York Hannah Blumenthal, Financial Analyst for Museum Affiliates; Oliver Dettler, Special Projects, Art Director; Betsy Ennis, Director of Public Affairs; Pepi Marchetti Franchi, Executive Associate to the Director; Kendall Hubert, Director of Corporate Development; and Helen Warwick, Director of Individual Giving and Membership; and in Las Vegas Anita Getzler, Head of Education; Sasha D. Jackowich, Public Affairs Manager; and Marcus Williams, Operations Manager.

This publication has benefited from the discriminating attention of Meghan Dailey, Associate Editor, and the clear-sighted design of Cassey L. Chou, Senior Graphic Designer in collaboration with Marcia Fardella, Chief Graphic Designer, and Christine Sullivan, Graphic Designer. Elizabeth Levy, Director of Publications; Elizabeth Franzen, Managing Editor; Tracy L. Hennige, Production Assistant, and editor Laura Morris have each offered their guidance and meticulousness in producing the exhibition's catalogue.

Susan Davidson
Curator, Guggenheim Museum

POP

Shaping Pop:
From Objects to Icons at the Guggenheim

Susan Davidson

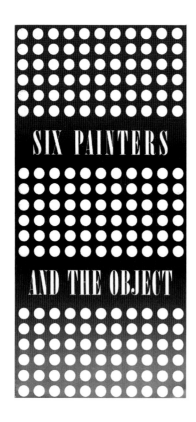

THE DECADE OF THE 1960s was one of the most provocative—culturally, politically, and philosophically—of the twentieth century. America had become an industrialized society poised on the brink of the information age. The remarkable economic growth that transpired from the end of the Second World War through the Cold War period of the 1950s resulted in a newly invigorated consumer culture in America.

A number of the artists who emerged, or more appropriately, burst upon the art world, particularly in New York and Los Angeles in the first years of the decade, were responding to this new commercialism. Indeed those who came to be identified as Pop artists embraced consumerism as a fitting subject of their art. Expression and gesture—hallmarks of Abstract Expressionism which preceded Pop in the late 1940s and early 1950s—were replaced with cool, detached, mechanical illustrations of common objects, often based on appropriated advertising images. Pop art was in fact proposing a new kind of subjectivity, one that did not rely on an artist's singular expressive gesture, the *main d'artiste*. While many of the Abstract Expressionists had turned hermetically inward, the Pop artists turned outward for aesthetic stimuli. Radically redefining the subject matter deemed suitable for aesthetic use, Pop art was a significant sociological phenomenon and a mirror of society. In turn, the consumer industry itself adopted Pop art as an antidote to the rigidity of "high art."

In Pop art, the narrative or epic impulse of Abstract Expressionism was replaced with straightforward depictions of the everyday, and the mass-produced was afforded the same significance as unique works of fine art; the gulf between "high art" and "low art" was gleefully eroded. Basing their techniques, style, and imagery on certain aspects of mass reproduction, media-derived imagery, and

consumer society, artists such as Jim Dine, Roy Lichtenstein, Claes Oldenburg, James Rosenquist, Andy Warhol, and Tom Wesselmann took inspiration from advertising, pulp magazines, billboards, movies, television, comic strips, and shop windows. Their images, presented with—and sometimes transformed by—humor, wit, and irony, may be read as both an unabashed celebration and a scathing critique of popular culture.

American Pop Icons features thirty-two paintings and sculptures from eight of the most important precursors to and participants in the Pop art movement—Dine, Jasper Johns, Lichtenstein, Oldenburg, Robert Rauschenberg, Rosenquist, Warhol, and Wesselmann. This concise overview takes as its starting point the Guggenheim's leading role among museums in bringing Pop art to a wider audience when it presented—at the height of the movement—the seminal exhibition *Six Painters and the Object* (March 14–June 12, 1963), organized by British art historian, curator, and critic Lawrence Alloway, and its accompanying catalogue (figs. 1 and 2). The Guggenheim would continue this tradition with monographic exhibitions for Lichtenstein, Dine, Oldenburg, Rauschenberg, Rosenquist, and Warhol in subsequent years.[1] Few of the artworks included in Alloway's exhibition are shown here, but the same spirit is unmistakably present. *American Pop Icons* showcases Pop art acquisitions made by the Guggenheim since *Six Painters and the Object*.[2] In addition, important loans are drawn from the collection of Ileana Sonnabend, who was one of the most significant Pop art collectors and gallerists, as well as from institutional and private lenders in the United States and Europe.

This exhibition references Alloway's timely Pop art show, organized at the very moment when the movement was so fresh that misconceptions and derision far outweighed acceptance. This current presentation has been expanded to include eight artists, rather than Alloway's original choice of six, and treats Rauschenberg and Johns as precursors to the movement rather than central practitioners.[3] Moreover, the addition of Oldenburg and Wesselmann here is an effort to close the gap on their omission from *Six Painters and the Object*.[4]

The term "Pop art" was first used in print by Alloway in 1958 to characterize the manifestations of popular culture (television, advertising, billboards, magazines) that were considered inferior to high culture.[5] Alloway, who was a member of the Independent Group[6]—an interdisciplinary group of British artists, architects, and critics—called for an art that would reflect contemporary experience and popular culture, would have a common interest in vernacular sources, and would share an aim to attack absolutist theories of art. The Independent Group organized four exhibitions, including the groundbreaking *This Is Tomorrow* (Whitechapel Art Gallery, London, 1956) where another one of its members, Richard Hamilton, presented his now-famous collage (originally made for the exhibition's poster and as a catalogue illustration) *Just what is it that makes today's homes so different, so appealing?* (1956), a seminal work that anticipated most aspects of Pop art. Signaling the dominance of American culture even in postwar-depressed London, Hamilton's sources were culled from American popular publications, such as *Life* magazine, brought to England by fellow artist John McHale. This seemingly nonsensical collage depicts a domestic interior engulfed in contemporary information transmission systems, including a movie marquee, telephones, tape recorders, televisions, etc. A standing muscleman holds a Tootsie Pop as if it were a tennis racket, while a scantily clad woman lounges on the sofa, ignoring her domestic duties. The nearly nude muscleman and his

voluptuous companion telegraph the erotic charge that modern advertising has attributed to acts of consumerism.

While its terminology and initial critical thinking originated in England, Pop art simultaneously arose in America where it would reach its fullest incarnation. Around the same time that the Independent Group was active, Rauschenberg proposed an alternative to the prevailing mode of art making in the United States. The diverse objects of Rauschenberg's celebrated Combine paintings fused two-dimensional painting with sculpture. Johns, playing on illusion and reality, repainted beer cans, targets, and the American flag, objects so iconic and commonplace that they required a new set of criteria to be viewed as artworks. The unique approach of Rauschenberg and Johns to the object paved the way for artists in the next decade. Oldenburg's configurations of functional objects like telephones and his enlarged soft sculptures of food, Roy Lichtenstein's borrowings from comic strips, James Rosenquist's billboard montages of banal media-derived images, and Andy Warhol's repetitions of images of celebrities and contemporary brand-name products all pushed subject matter to such prominence that it temporarily masked out formal considerations. As the art historian Leo Steinberg commented: "Our eyes will have to grow accustomed . . . to a new presence in art: the presence of subject matter absolutely at one with the form."[7] Many of these artists used commercial and mechanical processes such as photography or silkscreening, thus obtaining a flat rendering that denied any subjective emotion. Their work was snappy but detached—the epitome of cool.

In 1962, Thomas Messer, the Guggenheim's director, enticed Alloway to leave England permanently to become his principal curatorial appointment at the museum. It was Alloway's first curatorial job in America[8] and seemingly

FIGURE 2
Sylvia Sleigh and Lawrence Alloway, New York, ca. 1968. Photo: Vivien Campbell Stoll

a bold move on Messer's part to charge an Englishman with the task of "acquainting the museum's public with aspects of current American art."[9] Like his predecessor at the Guggenheim, James Johnson Sweeney, whose curatorial objectives encompassed a broader sensibility of Modern art, Alloway veered away from the founding director Hilla von Rebay's lifelong passion for the spiritual in art and her reliance on nonobjective painting and sculpture. Alloway's "liberal and broadly inclusive aesthetic orientation could not have been more dissimilar from Rebay's quest for the metaphysical essence of painting."[10] Yet the two were remarkably similar in their fundamental understanding of the art contemporary to their own time. Then as now, the Guggenheim's approach to the presentation of art encompasses a two-part objective, one aspect of which commemorates elements of the recent art-historical past; the other focuses on the immediate present with an eye toward future developments.[11] It was in this vein that Alloway, upon accepting his post,

immediately began work on the exhibition *Six Painters and the Object.* That Alloway would want to organize a Pop exhibition for the Guggenheim was not so improbable. He had been charged with raising the profile of the institution and what better way to do so than to show radical new art that had everyone talking—a movement with which he was already intimately engaged. Being a recent immigrant to America was no disadvantage for him.[12] In fact, he readily accepted American Pop art as a more successful phenomenon than its counterparts in England or France.

Intended to be the first museum exhibition devoted solely to this burgeoning trend in American art, *Six Painters and the Object,* was by the time it opened on March 14, 1963, in fact the second.[13] However, its importance cannot be underestimated. Of all the Pop art exhibitions that were organized in the 1960s, Alloway's was the only one that stressed the historical tradition of the movement. By underscoring the past, Alloway established a framework for Pop.

He established as influences the eighteenth-century prints of William Hogarth, the nineteenth-century engravings of Gustave Courbet, Post-Impressionist paintings by Vincent van Gogh and Paul Gauguin, and the earlier twentieth-century machine paintings of Fernand Léger. Moreover, *Six Painters and the Object* was the only Pop art exhibition of significance presented by a New York museum in the 1960s, a fact that went a long way toward legitimizing the activities of these artists. The exhibition generated an unusual amount of national press coverage, not only in art magazines but also in monthly news journals and on television.[14]

Prior to Alloway's Guggenheim exhibition, the art world was struggling to properly identify the new aesthetic it found itself confronted with. The speed with which Pop art excited the popular imagination was a corollary to the very brief period of time in which it initially flourished, from 1960 to 1964. Contrary to the adage that most great art is ignored for years, this new art quickly burst onto the scene, sparking so much interest and enthusiasm from critics, collectors, and gallery owners that even its moniker was much debated: New Realism, Popular Image Art, Common Object Art, Factualism, Neo Dadaism, American Dream Painting, Sign Painting, Anti-Sensibility Painting, and Cool-Art were just a few names put forth in an attempt to label the new art.[15] Pop art won out, being a short hand for popular culture that then evolved to describe the artistic expressions of that culture.[16]

It was actually a group of commercial art galleries that were the first to champion Pop art by presenting seemingly nonstop single-artist shows,[17] creating a buzz that in many cases generated immediate sales. Collectors—from taxi company owner Robert Scull (fig. 3) to insurance executive Leon Kraushar (fig. 4) to Burton and Emily Tremaine to Count Guiseppe Panza di Biumo—competed in a frenzied rush to acquire the best and latest of the new American art.[18] Kraushar, perhaps the gutsiest of the group and arguably the one who possessed the best eye proselytized in *Life* magazine: "Pop is the art of today, and tomorrow, and all the future.

FIGURE 4
Mrs. Leon Kraushar at home, ca. 1964, with Tom Wesselmann's *Bathtub Collage # 1* (1963) in foreground. Photo: Ken Heyman

These pictures are like IBM stock . . . and this is the time to buy."[19]

Both 1960 and 1961 were still emergent years for the mainstream's awareness of Pop art,[20] but by 1962, the movement was well established in the art world. Museums across the country were picking up on the new art and including representative artists in thematic group exhibitions. The first to include nearly all the Pop artists was Douglas MacAgy's *1961* exhibition for the Dallas Museum of Contemporary Arts (April 3–May 13, 1962), which included works by Dine (*A Universal Color Chart*), Lichtenstein (*The Kiss*), Johns (*Portrait—Viola Farber*), Rauschenberg (*Stripper*), and Rosenquist (*Shadows*), as well as a selection of soft sculptures from Oldenburg's *The Store*. Taking the year of creation as the basis for inclusion of each work, *1961* was a mixed bag of thirty-six artists that ranged from Joseph Albers to Robert Motherwell to Jack Youngerman, with a host of regional Texas artists, such as Joseph Glasco and Roy Fridge, thrown in for good measure. Despite the mélange, the exhibition successfully tracked the diversity of artistic expression at the moment. Not limiting himself to the visual arts, MacAgy commissioned a performance piece from Oldenburg, whose *Injun* was the first Happening to take place in a museum.[21]

Such avant-garde activity may seem at odds with the perception of Dallas as a cultural backwater, but MacAgy was a sophisticated transplant who had had an illustrious national career as both an art educator and museum director—he was someone with his finger on the pulse.[22]

Later that year, another prognosticator, Walter Hopps, curator of the Pasadena Museum of Art (now the Norton Simon Museum), assembled the first fully realized Pop art exhibition in the United States. (Alloway's Guggenheim exhibition would, nonetheless, have a greater impact on the national scene.) Hopps's exhibition was entitled *New Painting of Common Objects* (September 25–October 19, 1962) and included eight artists whose work he believed represented a common thread of the current avant-garde.[23] He featured the West Coast Pop painters Robert Dowd, Joe Goode, Phillip Hefferton, Ed Ruscha, and Wayne Thiebaud, whose work was less detached than the three Pop artists from New York—Dine, Lichtenstein, and Warhol—he included. Hopps's familiarity with the new art grew out of his years as cofounder, with assemblage artist Edward Keinholz, of the Ferus Gallery in Los Angeles. Like Alloway, Hopps had recently joined the staff of a museum and, also like Alloway, brought to the curatorial position a unique knowledge of contemporary art and an uncanny ability to refine this knowledge that continues to this day.[24] While important in the critical acceptance of the history of Pop art and despite the fact that it was the first, the Pasadena exhibition garnered little national attention save two idiosyncratic reviews that struggled with the mundane and banal concepts of consumerism that the exhibition presented.[25]

The latter months of 1962 brought many of the issues surrounding the legitimacy of Pop art to the fore. The Museum of Modern Art, New York, founded as the defender of Modern art, held a symposium that debated the merits of the style.[26]

FIGURE 5
Installation view of *International Exhibition of the New Realists* at the Sidney Janis Gallery's temporary annex, 19 West Fifty-seventh Street, New York, 1962. Works shown (left, near ceiling, to right): Daniel Spoerri, *la parc de Marcelle* (1961), Roy Lichtenstein, *Refrigerator* (1962), Martial Raysse, *Pump Torso* (1962), and Jim Dine, *Five Feet of Colorful Tools* (1962). Photo: Eric Pollitzer

Newspapers and periodicals devoted countless pages to the new American art, although most art critics were initially bemused or hostile.[27] With the exception of Alloway and Gene Swenson,[28] most believed that Pop art lacked metaphor and symbol, the very qualities that defined high art. In addition, commentators were appalled by the paintings' untransformed presentation of commercial subject matter, an aspect much debated at the Museum of Modern Art's symposium. The fact that the subject of this new art depicted familiar things, things they all knew, unsettled the art critics because it did not follow Modernism's prescriptions for aesthetic usage. Instead, Pop art glorified consumerism, a category traditionally considered lowbrow.

International Exhibition of the New Realists (November 1–December 1, 1962), the most critical gallery exhibition and the largest devoted exclusively to the emergent new art, was organized by the esteemed Sidney Janis Gallery in New York.[29] Well known for championing the work of Abstract Expressionist artists like Willem de Kooning, Jackson Pollock, and Mark Rothko—the very artists whose success the Pop group threatened—Janis's foray into the new art was something of a departure for the gallery. The exhibition presented Janis's interpretation of the worldwide activities of artists working under the Pop rubric, at that moment still unnamed.[30] One to three works each by fifty-four English, French, German, Italian, and American artists who were addressing the object as subject were assembled both in the gallery's two main rooms at 15 East Fifty-seventh Street, and in an empty storefront across Fifth Avenue from the gallery at 19 West Fifty-seventh Street, fully visible to midtown's busy city dwellers (fig. 5). Mimicking Oldenburg's *The Store* on the Lower Eastside, where the initiated and the uninitiated could wonder in off the street to purchase his then inexpensive sculptures of clothing (sneakers, pants, or shirts, ties, hats, etc.) or food

(doughnuts, candy bars, sandwiches, cakes, etc.), Janis's show "hit the New York art world with the force of an earthquake."[31]

Months before the Janis exhibition opened, Alloway formally proposed his Pop art exhibition to the Guggenheim's board of trustees. He envisioned an extravaganza that would fill "two ramps [of the museum's spiral] showing about forty-five artworks by a maximum of twenty artists from East and West coasts of U.S." and would "be sufficient to (a) demonstrate common features and (b) the diversity within the style."[32] Although Alloway had coined the term "Pop art" years earlier, he acknowledged that at this particular time (August 1962) the new art was still grappling with its identity, referring to his proposed exhibition as a "group show sampling a current trend: artists with no agreed-on name." Being the father of the term he considered exercising his propriety claim to title the exhibition "Pop Artists"; another possibility was "Signs and Objects," which more clearly defined his curatorial aim.[33] Both titles referred "to the popular sources that all these artist have in common, i.e., the mass media and the man-made environment." Alloway passionately argued that the time was ripe for such an exhibition, noting that "interest in art of this kind is increasing and as it increases so do misunderstandings about it." He cited Max Kozloff's contemporaneous article "'Pop' Culture, Metaphysical Disgust, and the New Vulgarians" as an example. "A seriously documented and carefully chosen show at this time would, I think, interest the public by its topicality and also define this area historically."

In his proposal, Alloway systematically established a classification of Pop imagery into four categories, placing specific artists in each:

1. Fully 3-D Objects (Rauschenberg and Oldenburg): found objects literally present and plastic simulacra; 2. Objects and Flat

Painting (Dine, Gene Beery, Ernst Trova, and
Alex Katz): anonymous artifacts and paintings
cut into figurative shapes; 3. Paintings of Objects
(Thiebaud, Peter Saul, Warhol, Rosenquist,
Stephenson [Harold Stevenson?], and Steven
Durkee): still life and mass production, graffiti
and abundance, Campbell Soup cans, Giantism,
and blow-ups of anatomical detail; and
4. Paintings of Signs (Johns, Lichtenstein,
Ramos, Allan D'Arcangelo, Billy Al Bengston,
Robert Indiana, and Ruscha): comic strips and
ads, comic strip heroes, Pop materials used
allegorically, and emblematic presentation.

Alloway wished to distinguish between object
makers, i.e., sculptors, and painters whose
subject matter was objects drawn from the
"communications network and the physical
environment of the city."[34] He perceived the
exhibition, when "historically viewed, [to be]
a compact section of a wider movement which
includes phases of Junk Culture, such as the
collage explosion and happenings. . . . My
preference is to stress . . . the painted imagery
rather than the objects." Alloway was clear in
his desire that the Guggenheim exhibition not
look like "Son of the Art of Assemblage," a
reference to William Seitz's groundbreaking
exhibition devoted to the history of collage and
sculptural works held at the Museum of Modern
Art the previous year.[35]

Most important, Alloway seemed to have an
insider's knowledge of which artists Janis
planned to include in his forthcoming gallery
exhibition, as well as how Janis intended to
present them. Alloway suspected that it would
be a jumble, referring to Janis's planned
exhibition in his proposal as a "sloppy survey."
For the Guggenheim exhibition, Alloway intended
that "the catalouge could be small but should
be packed with information" and "should
combine the kick of topicality with art historical
accuracy." Indeed, his essay for the *Six Painters*

and the Object catalogue fulfilled this intention,
becoming one of the most influential treatises
on the movement, written from the perspective
of a true insider.

In fact, Janis's exhibition did confuse matters in
its mixing of conceptual artists (Yves Klein and
Daniel Buren) and assemblage artists (Jean
Tinguely and Arman) with painters of common
objects and signs (Lichtenstein, Rosenquist,
and Warhol). In November, a few weeks after the
New Realist exhibition opened, Alloway sent a
memorandum to Messer, expressing concern
that there were too many Pop shows on view at
the moment, citing in New York, in addition to
Janis's anthology, Warhol and Indiana at Stable
Gallery and Oldenburg and Wesselmann at Green
Gallery, as well as group shows being planned
from Philadelphia to Pasadena. He nonetheless
was steadfast in his belief that a clear "definition
in opposition to the general confusion" would
not only be welcome but was needed. Messer
seconded his concern and urged him to press
ahead with his plans.[36]

When *Six Painters and the Object* opened in
mid-March, Alloway had narrowed his original
concept to feature six New York–based artists
with paintings by each that represented their
interpretation of the object. The exhibition was
installed in six of the eight bays on the top ramp
of the Guggenheim museum, with each bay
displaying five or six works of a single artist.
Alloway began with the work of Johns, followed
by that of Dine, Rauschenberg, Warhol,
Lichtenstein, and Rosenquist (fig. 7). It was
a compelling presentation and attendance
exceeded all expectations. Two thousand
copies of the catalogue were printed—an
unusually high number for the time. The book
was designed by Herbert Matter, whose work
for *Harper's Bazaar*, *Vogue*, and the furniture
maker Knoll made him a highly sought after
graphic designer.

The Guggenheim began plans to travel the exhibition even before the show opened in New York. Messer canvassed other museums, both large and small throughout North America. In his letter, he advocated that "it would not be too much to say that [the exhibition] will attempt to set right the mixed presentations that have occurred in many places by stressing the pure painting forms in separation from the crowded assemblages of objects and other tendencies with which these have often been associated."[37] The responses were staggeringly quick and conspicuously enthusiastic. The Jocelyn Art Museum in Omaha, Nebraska, perceived the exhibition as a "most timely ('hot') subject and wished to participate."[38] A number of the institutions who expressed interest had to be turned away;[39] there were only seven venues available for travel.[40] When the exhibition reached the Los Angeles County Museum of Art, Alloway expanded it to include six West Coast artists.[41] The lenders to the New York exhibition had been asked to part with their works for a year's tour. Most agreed, but a number did not, and Alloway was forced to make substitutions. Others were keen to come to the aid of the new art. John Weber of the Dwan Gallery, Los Angeles,

recognized that many lenders, having acquired their works within the last two years, might be reticent to extend their loans and therefore offered a couple of paintings from the gallery's inventory, namely, Lichtenstein's *Tzing* from the *Live Ammo* series (1962) and Dine's large *Pink Bathroom* (1962).[42] As a result, the traveling exhibition was significantly different, although just as formidable.

As a self-contained movement Pop art had dissipated by the end of the 1960s. The current work of many of its early practitioners has moved away from purely Pop statements but continues to provide lively commentary on contemporary culture. Once considered a radical departure, their art has been thoroughly assimilated by the very consumer culture that it initially critiqued. In 1963, when the work was still considered risky, the Guggenheim staged the small but momentous *Six Painters and the Object*.[43] The endorsement that the Guggenheim bestowed upon Pop art at that critical juncture validated the movement and, in turn, demonstrated the museum's leadership in establishing artistic trends.

FIGURE 7
Installation view of James Rosenquist paintings included in *Six Painters and the Object* at the Solomon R Guggenheim Museum, New York, 1963. Works shown (left to right): *4-1949 Guys*, *Mayfair*, and *The Lines Were Deeply Etched on the Map of Her Face* (all 1962). Photo: James Rosenquist

NOTES

1. In New York, Lichtenstein received monographic shows at the Guggenheim in 1969 and 1993–94, and a Dine exhibition featuring work from 1959 to 1969 was presented in 1999. At the behest of the Guggenheim, the Deutsche Guggenheim Berlin commissioned and exhibited in 1998 Rosenquist's *The Swimmer in the Econo-mist* (1997–98), a three-part contemporary history painting. Oldenburg in 1995–96, Rauschenberg in 1997–98, and Rosenquist forthcoming in 2003–04 had retrospectives organized for the Guggenheim in New York, which included national and international itineraries. Warhol was featured in several exhibitions, including one devoted to his Factory years (Guggenheim Museo Bilbao, 1999–2000) and another to his series of *Last Supper* paintings (Guggenheim Museum Soho, 1998).

2. The Guggenheim's collection includes additional works by each of the eight artists featured in *American Pop Icons*, in addition to works by other Pop artists, such as Billy Al Bengston, Mel Ramos, Larry Rivers, Ed Ruscha, and George Segal.

3. Barbara Rose was the first to identify the work of Rauschenberg and Johns as not necessarily Pop: "it is not as inappropriate to talk of them in the same breath as it is to associate them with 'pop art,' which has a lot to do with them, but with which they have nothing to do." Barbara Rose, "Pop Art at the Guggenheim," *Art International* (Lugano) 7, no. 5 (May 25, 1963), pp. 20–22. Art history has since correctly assumed this position in regard to Rauschenberg and Johns, e.g., see *Hand-Painted Pop: American Art in Transition 1955–1962*, exh. cat. (Los Angeles: Museum of Contemporary Art, 1993).

4. Both were included in Alloway's original exhibition prospectus but did not make the final cut. Whether this was due to space limitations—the sixth and top ramp of the Guggenheim spiral only has eight bays, and two were used for storage while the other six bays each showed the work of one artist—or was a curatorial decision is unknown.

5. See Lawrence Alloway, "The Arts and The Mass Media," *Architectural Design* (London) 28 (Feb. 1958), pp. 84–85.

6. For more on the Independent Group, see David Robbins, *The Independent Group: Postwar Britain and the Aesthetics of Plenty* (Cambridge: MIT Press, 1990); and Lynne Cooke, "The Independent Group: British and American Pop Art, A 'Palimpcestuous' Legacy," in Kirk Varnedoe and Adam Gopnik, eds., *Modern Art and Popular Culture: Readings in High and Low* (New York: Museum of Modern Art, 1999).

7. Leo Steinberg, comments at "A Symposium on Pop Art," the Museum of Modern Art, New York, Dec. 13, 1962, from proceedings published in *Arts Magazine* (New York) 37, no. 8 (Apr. 1963), p. 40.

8. Previously, Alloway had been deputy director of London's Institute of Contemporary Art from 1954 to 1957. While at the Guggenheim, he organized nearly twenty exhibitions, including *Word and Image* (Dec. 8, 1965–Jan. 2, 1966), *Barnett Newman: The Stations of the Cross: lema sbachthani* (Apr. 23–June 19, 1966), and *Systemic Painting* (Sept. 21–Nov. 27, 1966). He resigned from the museum in 1966 after clashing with Messer over what the Guggenheim was to exhibit at the Venice Biennale. Alloway has written extensively on Pop art and the art of his time. From 1968 to 1981 he was a professor of art history at the State University of New York at Stony Brook. His principal essays are collected under the title *Network: Art and the Complex Present* (Ann Arbor: UMI Research Press, 1984). He died on January 2, 1990, and is survived by his wife, the artist Sylvia Sleigh. See *An Unnerving Romanticism: The Art of Sylvia Sleigh and Lawrence Alloway*, exh. cat. (Philadelphia: Philadelphia Art Alliance, 2001).

9. Press release issued to announce Alloway's resignation from the Guggenheim, June 13, 1966, Rosalind Constable papers, Menil Archives, Houston.

10. Nancy Spector, "Against the Grain: A History of Contemporary Art at the Guggenheim," *Art of This Century: The Guggenheim Museum and Its Collection* (New York: Guggenheim Museum, 1997), p. 233.

11. Ibid., p. 232.

12. Alloway received a four-month Foreign Leader's grant from the United States government to study American painting in 1958, which was his first visit. He met many influential people in the art world at that time, including the critic and art historian Eugene Goosen, who invited him for a one-year academic appointment in art history at Bennington College, Vermont (1961–62).

13. Walter Hopps's *New Painting of Common Objects*, held at the Pasadena Museum of Art (Sept. 25–Oct. 19, 1962), was the first such museum exhibition.

14. Some of the most important reviews include "Pop Art: Cult of the Commonplace," *Time*, May 3, 1963, pp. 60–70; "Art: Pop. Pop," *Time*, Aug. 30, 1963, p. 40; Don Factor, "*Six Painters and the Object* and *Six More*, L.A. County Museum of Art," *Artforum* (San Francisco) 2, no. 3 (Sept. 1963), pp. 13–14; Leonard Horowitz, "Art: Six Characters in Search of an Art Movement," *The Village Voice*, Apr. 4, 1963, p. 11; Donald Judd, "New York Exhibitions: In the Galleries–Six Painters and the Object," *Arts Magazine* (New York) 37, no. 9 (May–June 1963), pp. 108–09; Stuart Preston, "On Display: All-Out Series of Pop Art: *Six Painters and the Object* Exhibited at Guggenheim," *The New York Times*, Mar. 21, 1963, p. 8; and Barbara Rose, "Pop Art at the Guggenheim," *Art International* (Lugano) 7, no. 5 (May 1963), pp. 20–22. Emily Genauer, the most respected art critic of the time, appeared on NBC television on March 14, 1963. As she walked through the Guggenheim, she compared the Pop artists to nineteenth-century American sign painters, American artist Stuart Davis, and contemporary advertisements. This sort of historical analysis would have pleased Alloway immensely.

15. March 1962 seems to be when the name "Pop" was settled upon. See Max Kozloff, "'Pop' Culture, Metaphysical Disgust, and the New Vulgarians," *Art International* (Lugano) 6, no. 2 (Mar. 1962), pp. 35–36. The list of other terms is taken from Sidra Stich, *Made in USA: An Americanization in Modern Art, The '50s and 60s* (Berkeley: University of California Press, 1987), p. 2.

16. The term "Pop" was misapplied to Johns and Rauschenberg, and artists such as Dine and Rosenquist bristled at the label even as their inclusion in the movement significantly accelerated their careers.

17. In New York, 1962 began with a Dine show at Martha Jackson (Jan. 9–Feb. 3); then, came the first one-person shows of Rosenquist at the Green Gallery, (Jan. 30–Feb. 17) and Lichtenstein at Leo Castelli (Feb. 10–Mar. 3). Warhol's *Thirty-two Campbell's Soup Cans* were exhibition at the Ferus Gallery, Los Angeles (July 9–Aug. 4). The fall season in New York opened with Oldenburg's soft sculptures at the Green Gallery (Sept. 24–Oct. 20), followed by Sidney Janis's *International Exhibition of the New Realists* (Nov. 1–Dec. 1). The year concluded with Warhol's first New York exhibition at the Stable Gallery (Nov. 6–24), Wesselmann's *Great American Nudes* at the Green Gallery(Nov. 13–Dec. 1), and a group show of thirteen artists, *My Country 'Tis of Thee* (Nov. 18–Dec. 15) at the Dwan Gallery, Los Angeles.

18. The Scull collection was sold at auction in 1973 when Robert and his wife Ethel divorced. Upon Krausher's death in 1967, his wife sold the collection to the German industrialist Karl Ströher, who died in 1988; Sotheby's sold the bulk of this collection in May 1989. The Tremaine collection was sold at auction in 1988 and 1991, while many Pop artworks from the Panza collection were sold to the Museum of Contemporary Art, Los Angeles, in 1984. Both the Sculls and the Tremaines were significant lenders to the *Six Painters and the Object* exhibition.

19. "You Bought It—Now Live with It," *Life*, July 16, 1965, p. 59.

20. Four exhibitions in New York during these years greatly influenced the course of Pop art: *New Media–New Forms I* (June 6–24, 1960) and *New Media–New Forms, Version 2* (Sept. 27–Oct. 22, 1960) at the Martha Jackson Gallery, *Environments–Situations–Spaces* (May 25–June 23, 1961) at the Martha Jackson and David Anderson galleries, and *The Art of Assemblage* (Oct. 2–Nov. 12, 1961) at the Museum of Modern Art.

21. *Injun*, a film of Oldenburg's work made by Roy Fridge in Dallas, was one of the first recordings of a Happening. For a history of performance art, see Barbara Haskell, *Blam! The Explosion of Pop, Minimalism, and Performance 1958–1964*, exh. cat. (New York: W. W. Norton; the Whitney Museum of American Art, 1984).

22. For an excellent study of MacAgy's career, see David Beasley, *Douglas MacAgy and the Foundations of Modern Art Curatorship* (Simcoe, Ontario: Davus Publishing, 1998).

23. See Jim Edwards's interview with Walter Hopps, in David Brauer et al., *Pop Art: U.S./U.K. Connections, 1956–1966*, exh. cat. (Houston: The Menil Collection, 2001); see pp. 42–54 for Hopps's personal recollection of *New Painting of Common Objects*.

24. In a move similar to Messer's in 1962, Thomas Krens, the Guggenheim's current director, invited Walter Hopps to be senior adjunct curator of contemporary art in 2001. In this capacity, he recently organized, with Sarah Bancroft, a Rosenquist retrospective for the museum that will tour internationally. At the Guggenheim, he was also the co-curator (with this author) of the Rauschenberg retrospective in 1997. After leaving the Pasadena Museum of Art in 1967, Hopps became director of the Corcoran Gallery of Art, Washington, D.C., from 1967 to 1972, then a curator at the National Collection of Fine Arts (now Smithsonian American Art Museum), Washington, D.C., from 1972 to 1979, and director of the Menil Collection, Houston, from 1980 to 1988, where he is also presently curator of contemporary art.

25. See John Coplans, "The New Paintings of Common Objects," *Artforum* (Los Angeles) 1, no. 6 (Nov. 1962), pp. 26–29; and Jules Langsner, "Los Angeles Letter," *Art International* (Lugano) 6, no. 9 (Sept. 1962), p. 49.

26. "A Symposium on Pop Art" was held at the Museum of Modern Art, New York, Dec. 13, 1962. The proceedings were published in a special issue of *Arts Magazine* (New York) 37, no. 7 (Apr. 1963), pp. 36–45. Participants included Dore Ashton, Henry Geldzahler, Hilton Kramer, Stanley Kunitz, Leo Steinberg, and moderator Peter Selz.

27. These critics included Dore Ashton, John Canaday, Clement Greenberg, Thomas Hess, Max Kozloff, Hilton Kramer, Irving Sandler, and Peter Selz. It may be that at the time they were peeved for not being the first to signal the new art. Typically, it is the critics enthusiasm, not the public's, that validates artistic styles.

28. See Gene Swenson, "The New American 'Sign Painters,'" *Art News* (New York) 61, no. 5 (Sept. 1962), pp. 44–47, 60–62, and his two-part article, "What is Pop Art?" *Art News* (New York) 62, no. 7 (Nov. 1963, Part I), pp. 24–27, 60–65; and 62, no. 10 (Feb. 1964, Part II), pp. 40–43, 62–67.

29. For an in-depth look at the importance of *International Exhibition of the New Realists*, see Bruce Altshuler, "Pop Triumphant: A New Realism" *The Avant-Garde in Exhibition: New Art in the Twentieth Century* (New York: Harry N. Abrams, 1994), pp. 212–19.

30. For the title of the exhibition, Janis chose "New Realists," a translation of the French term favored by Pierre Restany. However, in his essay "On the Theme of the Exhibition" in the catalogue, Janis preferred the name "Factual Artists." *International Exhibition of the New Realists*, exh. cat. (New York: Sidney Janis Gallery, 1962).

31. Harold Rosenberg, "The Art Galleries: The Game of Illusion," *The New Yorker*, Nov. 24, 1962, p. 162.

32. This and the following quotes are taken from Alloway's memorandum to Messer of Aug. 28, 1962, *Six Painters and the Object* curatorial files, Guggenheim Archive, New York.

33. Alloway would have the opportunity to use the title later for his second chapter in the *American Pop Art*, exh. cat. (New York: Collier, with the Whitney Museum of American Art, 1974).

34. Lawrence Alloway, *Six Painters and the Object*, exh. cat (New York: Guggenheim Museum, 1963), p. 7. This quote was also used in the press release announcing the exhibition.

35. *The Art of Assemblage* (Oct. 2–Nov. 12, 1961) greatly influenced a number of younger artists, including Rosenquist. See Julia Blaut, "James Rosenquist: Collage and the Painting of Modern Life," in *James Rosenquist: A Retrospective*, exh. cat. (New York: Guggenheim Museum, 2003), pp. 16–43.

36. Alloway memorandum to Messer, Nov. 14, 1962, *Six Painters and the Object* curatorial files.

37. Messer's form letter of Feb. 7, 1963, *Six Painters and the Object* curatorial files.

38. Richard Ahlborn to Messer, Feb. 14, 1963, *Six Painters and the Object* curatorial files.

39. The interested institutions not included in the tour were the Jocelyn Art Museum, Omaha, Nebraska; Art Gallery of Toronto; San Francisco Museum of Art; Wadsworth Athenaeum, Hartford; Saint Louis Museum of Art; and Addison Gallery of American Art, Andover, Massachusetts, among others.

40. In 1963, the *Six Painters and the Object* traveled to the Los Angeles County Museum of Art (July 24–Aug. 25), where it was augmented with the exhibition *Six More*. The second stop on the tour was the Minneapolis Institute of Arts (Sept. 3–29), followed by the University of Michigan, Ann Arbor (Oct. 9–Nov. 3), the Poses Art Institute, Brandeis University, Waltham, Massachusetts (Nov. 18–Dec. 29), the Carnegie Institute, Pittsburgh (Jan. 17–Feb. 23, 1964), the Columbus Gallery of Fine Arts, Columbus, Ohio (Mar. 8–Apr. 5), and the Art Center, La Jolla, California (Apr. 20–May 17, 1964).

41. The companion exhibition *Six More* featured the work of the West Coast Pop painters Billy Al Bengston, Joe Goode, Phillip Hefferton, Mel Ramos, Ed Ruscha, and Wayne Thiebaud. Alloway contributed the catalogue essay.

42. See John Weber to Alloway, April 27, 1963, *Six Painters and the Object* curatorial files. In the end, the Dine painting was not included.

43. In addition to *Six Painters and the Object*, 1963 also witnessed the following Pop art shows: *Pop Goes the Easel*, organized by Douglas MacAgy for the Contemporary Arts Museum, Houston (Apr. 4–30), *The Popular Image Exhibition*, organized by Alice Denney for the Washington Gallery of Modern Art, Washington, D.C. (Apr. 18–June 2), *Pop Art USA*, organized by John Coplans for the Oakland Art Museum (Sept. 7–29), *Popular Art: Artistic Projections of Common American Symbols* at the Nelson Gallery-Atkins Museum in Kansas City (Apr. 28–May 26), which traveled to the Albright-Knox Art Gallery, Buffalo (Nov. 19–Dec. 15), and *Signs of the Times III: Painting by Twelve Contemporary Pop Artists* at the Des Moines Art Center (Dec.–Jan. 1964).

POP
Plates

PLATE 1
Jasper Johns
Flags, 1987
Encaustic and newspaper on canvas
25½ x 33 inches
Collection of the artist

PLATE 2
Jasper Johns
Flashlight I, 1958
Sculp-metal over flashlight and wood
$5\frac{1}{4}$ x $9\frac{1}{8}$ x $3\frac{7}{8}$ inches
Sonnabend Collection

PLATE 3
Jasper Johns
Figure 8, 1959
Encaustic on canvas
$20\frac{1}{16}$ x 15 inches
Sonnabend Collection

PLATE 4
Jasper Johns
Fool's House, 1962
Oil on canvas with broom, fabric, wood,
and porcelain cup
72 x 36 inches
Collection of Jean Christophe Castelli

PLATE 6
Robert Rauschenberg
Dylaby, 1962
Combine painting: oil, wood, and metal on
canvas tarpaulin
9 feet 1½ inches x 7 feet 3 inches x 1 foot 3 inches
Sonnabend Collection

PLATE 7

Robert Rauschenberg

Barge, 1962–63

Oil and silkscreened ink on canvas

6 feet 7⅞ inches x 32 feet 2 inches

Solomon R. Guggenheim Museum, New York,

and Guggenheim Museum Bilbao

Additional funds contributed by Thomas H. Lee and
Ann Tenenbaum; the International Director's Council and
Executive Committee Members; and funds from
additional donors: Ulla Dreyfus-Best, Norma and Joseph
Saul Philanthropic Fund, Elizabeth Rea, Eli Broad, Dakis
Joannou, Peter Norton, Peter Lawson-Johnston, Michael
Wettach, Peter Littmann, Tiqui Atencio, Bruce and Janet
Karatz, and Giulia Ghirardi Pagliai
97.4566

PLATE 8
Robert Rauschenberg
Untitled, 1963
Oil, silkscreened ink, metal, and plastic on canvas
82 x 48 x 6¼ inches
Solomon R. Guggenheim Museum, New York
Purchased with funds contributed by Elaine and Werner
Dannheisser and The Dannheisser Foundation
82.2912

PLATE 9
Jim Dine
Shoe, 1961
Oil on canvas with wood
64½ x 56 inches
Sonnabend Collection

SHOE

PLATE 10
Jim Dine
Pearls, 1961
Oil, metallic paint, and rubber balls on canvas
70 x 60 inches
Solomon R. Guggenheim Museum, New York
Gift, Leon A. Mnuchin
63.1681

PEARLS

PLATE 11
Jim Dine
Four Soap Dishes, 1962
Oil on canvas with four metal soap dishes and painted
wooden soaps
48 x 40 inches
Sonnabend Collection

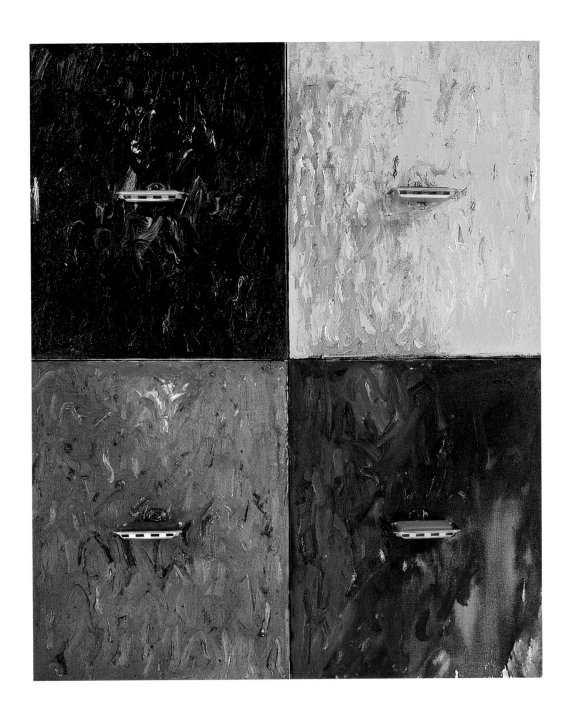

PLATE 12
Jim Dine
Summer Tools, 1962
Oil, tools, string, metal, glue bottles, and plastic
light fixture on three joined canvases
80 x 108 inches
Private collection

PLATE 14
Roy Lichtenstein
Compositions II, 1964
Oil on canvas
54 x 47¼ inches
Sonnabend Collection

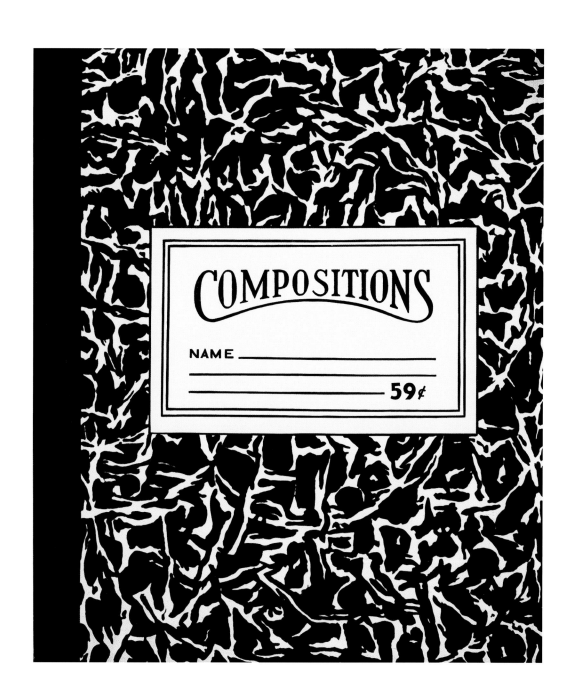

PLATE 16
Roy Lichtenstein
Preparedness, 1968
Oil and Magna on three joined canvases
10 x 18 feet
Solomon R. Guggenheim Museum, New York
69.1885.a-.c

54

PLATE 17
Claes Oldenburg
Soft Pay-Telephone, 1963
Vinyl filled with kapok, mounted on painted
wood panel
46½ x 19 x 9 inches
Solomon R. Guggenheim Museum, New York
Gift, Ruth and Philip Zierler in memory of their dear
departed son, William S. Zierler
80.2747

PLATE 18
Claes Oldenburg
Soft Light Switches—"Ghost" Version, 1963
Liquitex and graphite on canvas filled with kapok,
mounted on canvas over wood
52 x 52 x 9½ inches
The Berardo Collection,
Sintra Museum of Modern Art, Portugal

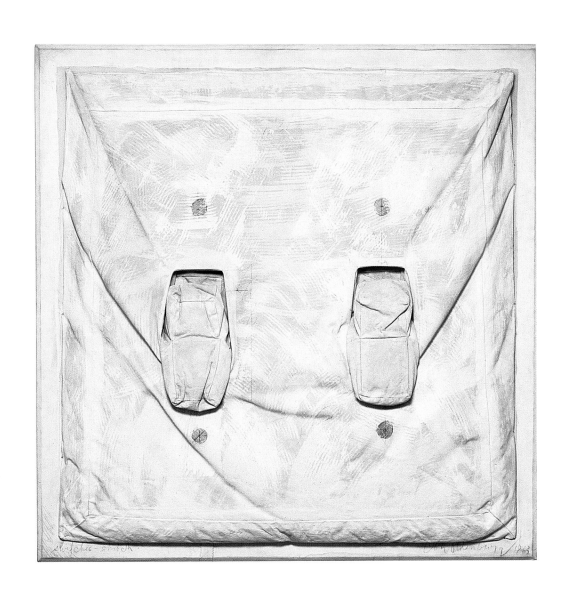

PLATE 19
James Rosenquist
Balcony, 1961
Oil on canvas and Plexiglas, with mirror
5 feet x 6 feet 1 inch
Sonnabend Collection

PLATE 20
James Rosenquist
Coentis Slip Studio, 1961
Oil on shaped canvas
34 x 43 inches
Collection of the artist

PLATE 21
James Rosenquist
The Facet, 1978
Oil on canvas
7 feet 6 inches x 8 feet
Lilja Art Fund Foundation, Basel
On deposit to Musée d'Art Moderne et d'Art
Contemporain, Nice

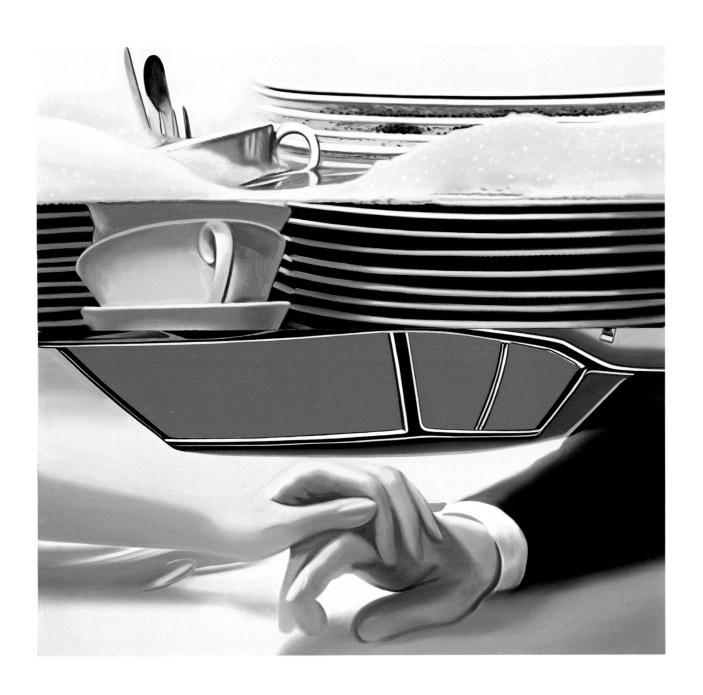

PLATE 22
James Rosenquist
The Meteor Hits the Swimmer's Pillow, 1997
Oil on linen, with metal bedsprings
8 feet x 5 feet 9 inches
Courtesy Bernard Jacobson Gallery, London

PLATE 24
Andy Warhol
Flowers, 1964
Silkscreened ink on canvas
81 x 81 inches
Sonnabend Collection

PLATE 25
Andy Warhol
Early Colored Liz (Chartreuse), 1963
Silkscreened ink on canvas
40 x 40 inches
Sonnabend Collection

PLATE 26
Andy Warhol
Early Colored Liz (Turquoise), 1963
Silkscreened ink on canvas
40 x 40 inches
Sonnabend Collection

PLATE 27
Andy Warhol
Orange Disaster #5, 1963
Acrylic and silkscreened enamel on canvas
8 feet 10 inches x 6 feet 9½ inches
Solomon R. Guggenheim Museum, New York
Gift, Harry N. Abrams Family Collection
74.2118

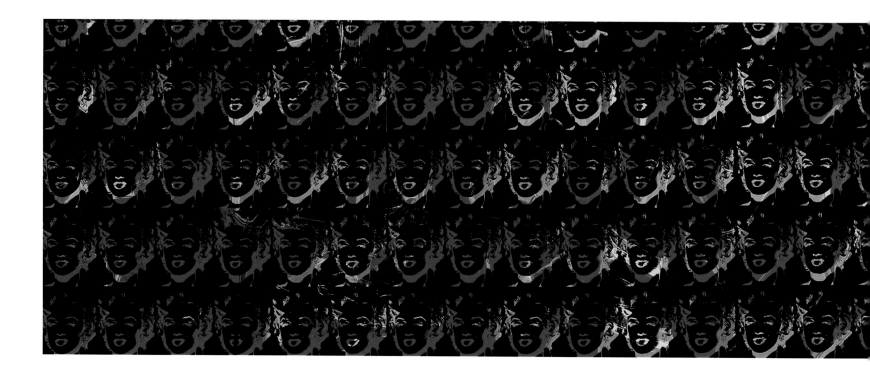

PLATE 28
Andy Warhol
One Hundred and Fifty Multicolored Marilyns, 1979
Acrylic and silkscreened enamel on canvas
6 feet 6 inches x 34 feet 6 inches
Guggenheim Museum Bilbao
1997.19

PLATE 29
Tom Wesselmann
Still Life #45, 1962
Oil, printed reproductions, and plastic relief on canvas
35 x 48 inches
Sonnabend Collection

PLATE 30
Tom Wesselmann
Still Life #21, 1962
Acrylic and printed reproductions on board,
with concealed tape recorder
48 x 60 inches
Private collection

PLATE 31
Tom Wesselmann
Still Life #34, 1963
Acrylic and printed reproductions on panel
47½ inches in diameter
Private collection

PLATE 32
Tom Wesselmann
Still Life #33, 1963
Oil and printed reproductions on three joined canvases
11 x 15 feet
Private collection

POP

Biographies and Catalogue Entries

Jim Dine

b. 1935

Jim Dine was born June 16, 1935, in Cincinnati, Ohio. He studied at night at the Cincinnati Art Academy during his senior year of high school and then attended the University of Cincinnati, the School of the Museum of Fine Arts, Boston, and Ohio University, Athens, from which he received his B.F.A. in 1957. Dine moved to New York in 1959 and soon became a pioneer creator of Happenings together with Allan Kaprow, Claes Oldenburg, Robert Whitman and others. He exhibited at the Judson Gallery, New York, in 1958 and 1959, and his first solo show took place at the Reuben Gallery, New York, in 1960.

Dine is closely associated with the development of Pop art in the early 1960s. Frequently he affixed everyday objects, such as tools and rope, shoes, neckties, and other articles of clothing, and even a bathroom sink to his canvases. Characteristically, these objects were Dine's personal possessions. This autobiographical content was evident in Dine's early *Crash* series of 1959–60, and appeared as well in subsequent bodies of work, such as the *Palettes*, *Hearts*, and bathrobe *Self-Portraits*. Dine has also made a number of three-dimensional works and environments, and is well-known for his drawings and prints. He has written and illustrated several books of poetry.

In 1965 Dine was a guest lecturer at Yale University, New Haven, and artist-in-residence at Oberlin College, Ohio. He was a visiting artist at Cornell University, Ithaca, New York, in 1967. From 1967 to 1971 he and his family lived in London. Dine has been given numerous solo shows in museums in Europe and the United States. In 1970 the Whitney Museum of American Art, New York, organized a major retrospective of his work, and in 1978 the Museum of Modern Art, New York, presented a retrospective of his etchings. Dine resides in New York and Putney, Vermont.

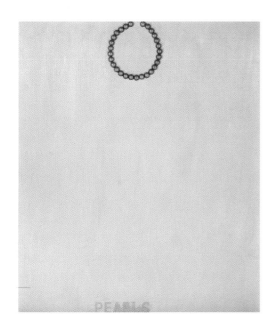

PLATE 10

Pearls, 1961
Oil, metallic paint, and rubber balls on canvas
70 x 60 inches
Solomon R. Guggenheim Museum, New York
Gift, Leon A. Mnuchin
63.1681

During the early 1960s Jim Dine was part of a loosely affiliated group of artists—including Red Grooms, Claes Oldenburg, and Lucas Samaras—who extended the gestural and subjective implications of Abstract Expressionist painting into outrageous performances, subsequently known as Happenings. Inspired by John Cage's radical approach to musical composition, which involved chance, indeterminacy, and an emphatic disregard for all artistic boundaries, they sought to transgress preexisting aesthetic values. Dine and Oldenburg brought this sensibility to bear on a two-artist exhibition called *Ray-Gun*, held at the Judson Gallery in New York in February and March 1960. For the show each artist made an installation consisting of a chaotic configuration of found and manipulated objects. In Dine's jumbled environment, *The House*, the walls and ceiling of the gallery were effaced by an agglomeration of painted cloth, fragmented domestic objects, scrawled slogans, crumbled paper, and suspended metal bedsprings. Scattered throughout were cardboard signs spelling out various household platitudes, such as "breakfast is ready" and "go to work." Dine claimed that the juxtaposition of these and other banal phrases with the surrounding domestic wreckage revealed the potential

violence inherent to a home. His critique of the myth of the happy home was amplified by anthropomorphic references—painted eyes, faces, and other body parts—that were hidden or lost amid the detritus.

A year later Dine began making paintings of discrete items—a hat, a necktie, and the necklace in *Pearls*, composed of rubber-ball halves covered with metallic paint. Although often construed as Pop art emblems, these paintings, which include the names of the depicted objects and in some cases collage elements, are more conceptually oriented than the playful and bold appropriations of popular imagery made by Roy Lichtenstein, James Rosenquist, and Andy Warhol. By so blatantly and provocatively combining word, image, and object, Dine invited an investigation into the presumed difference between representation and reality, the construction of meaning, and the arbitrary nature of language.—NS

PLATE 9

Shoe, 1961
Oil on canvas with wood
64½ x 56 inches
Sonnabend Collection

In 1961 Jim Dine's already introspective canvases began to feature a highly personal selection of both real and depicted articles of clothing, such as thickly impastoed ties, the front of a gargantuan coat, or an oversized bandanna. Embracing the array of textures and patterns offered by different fabrics, Dine employed dress as a means to project to the world a range of constructed identities while protecting his inner self from full exposure. His early assemblage *Green Suit* (1959) incorporated the artist's own corduroy suit and a phallic bulge to suggest Dine's absent body. In his five performance pieces from throughout the 1960s, the artist often appeared in outlandish garments—wearing a pigment-drenched painter's smock and clown makeup while performing as *The Smiling Workman* (1960), for example—that emphasized the constructed nature of his various routines.[1]

Dine's use of quotidian objects led to his critical association with the burgeoning American Pop art movement during this time, but the artist himself avoided such a classification, saying, "Pop is concerned with exteriors. I'm concerned with interiors."[2] His individual aesthetic was in opposition to the type of mechanically reproduced images appropriated from American mass culture that were freely used with a cool sense of irony by his contemporaries Andy Warhol and Tom Wesselmann. Taking as his point of departure the Abstract Expressionists' preoccupation with the transcendent qualities of paint, Dine focused upon the physicality of the canvas and applied his brushstrokes to the surface almost as if they were objects in order to achieve a particularly visceral aesthetic.

As a result of a psychological crisis, which began in 1961, Dine began to undergo psychoanalysis and led a quiet existence. Completed within this period of isolation and self reflection, *Shoe* serves as both a reminder and a validation of the artist's difficult childhood. "I was trying to reconstruct a history for myself of where I came from,"[3] the artist has explained, and the brown-and-white oxford evokes the elegant attire of Fred Astaire that was admired during Dine's youth. The accompanying textual label underscores the free association behind Dine's creative process ("I would just say 'shoe,' and I made *Shoe*,"[4] he remembered) while emphasizing the deliberately naive, childlike character of the composition.[5] Interested in the oscillation between reality and artifice as a means of exploring his own awareness of the extant world,[6] Dine affixed an actual wood shelf to the bottom edge of the painting. Such an addition emphasizes the self-referential nature of the canvas; the painting does not depict an image of a shoe, but rather the artist's own memory making.—KVW

1. On the relation between dress, self, and the body in Dine's work, see Germano Celant, "I Love What I'm Doing: Jim Dine, 1959–1969," in Celant and Clare Bell, *Jim Dine: Walking Memory, 1959–1969*, exh. cat. (New York: Guggenheim Museum, 1999), pp. 17–19.

2. John Gruen, "All Right, Jim Dine, Talk!" *New York: The World Journal Tribune Magazine* (Nov. 20, 1966), p. 34

3. From an interview with Dine in Celant and Bell, *Jim Dine: Walking Memory*, p. 116.

4. Ibid.

5. Alan Solomon, "Jim Dine and the Psychology of the New Art," *Art International* (Lugano) 8, no. 8 (Oct. 20, 1964), p. 54.

6. Celant and Bell, *Jim Dine: Walking Memory*, p. 63.

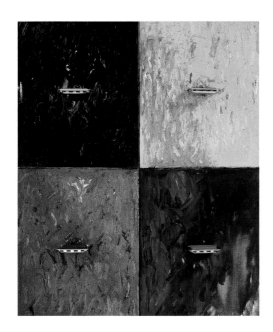

PLATE 11

Four Soap Dishes, 1962
Oil on canvas with four metal soap dishes and painted wooden soaps
48 x 40 inches
Sonnabend Collection

In the summer of 1962, bathroom fixtures such as medicine chests, towel racks, and sinks began to appear as elements in Dine's paintings. Culled directly from an abundantly stocked hardware store in East Hampton, New York, where Dine and his family spent time, such items narrated the artist's personal history: As a young boy in Cincinnati, Dine spent his summer weekends working in hardware stores owned by his grandfather and father. He found the array of goods on display to be a formative aesthetic experience, identifying a sculptural beauty in mundane objects. His *Bathroom* series mines his memories and associated emotions and creates what might be considered oblique self-portraits with anonymous objects employed as bodily substitutions.[1]

To structure these paintings, Dine looked to the geometric rigidity found in Piet Mondrian's crisp arrangements of lines and rectangles executed in primary colors.[2] A sense of this orderliness is present in one work from the *Bathroom* series, *Four Soap Dishes*, in which the gleaming metal trays cradling painted wood "soaps" extend from square patches of red, blue, yellow, and blackish green. Critic David Shapiro has suggested that such a grid, painted with agitated brushstrokes that remain confined within their rectilinear boundaries, provides a wry commentary upon the rigorous color theories of Josef Albers, which were ubiquitous within American art schools by the 1960s.[3] The blocks of color may also recall the commercial color charts created to detail available hues of house paint (another reference to the hardware stores of the artist's youth). Dine began an exploration of this format in his *Color Chart* series during the following year.

In Dine's *Bathroom* paintings, elements are often arranged to imply a larger environment just beyond the picture plane, with the canvas suggesting a wall that extends indefinitely. Reflective surfaces such as mirrored cabinets directly engage viewers in the works,[4] a condition that is subtly present in *Four Soap Dishes*, which enticingly proffers its colorful soaps. Like Dine's earlier installation *The House* (1960), a chaotic accumulation of found objects and detritus juxtaposed with newly constructed artworks, the *Bathroom* paintings were not intended to mimic a comfortable and realistic domestic environment, but rather to envelop viewers within their phantasmal setting drawn from the artist's own memories. Firmly rooted in the artistic realm, Dine's work was separate in intention from the assemblage constructions of Jasper Johns and Robert Rauschenberg, with whom he was often compared. Rejecting their conviction to merge art and life, Dine instead noted, "I think life comes to art but if the object is used, then people say the object is used to bridge that gap—it's crazy. The object is used to make art, just like paint is used to make art."[5]—KVW

1. Germano Celant and Clare Bell, *Jim Dine: Walking Memory, 1959–1969*, exh. cat. (New York: Guggenheim Museum, 1999), p. 156.

2. Ibid.

3. David Shapiro, *Jim Dine: Painting What One Is* (New York: Harry N. Abrams, 1981), p. 27.

4. Graham W. J. Beal, "Something to Hang Paint On," in *Jim Dine: Five Themes*, exh. cat. (Minneapolis: Walker Art Center, 1984), p. 17.

5. Gene Swenson, "What Is Pop Art?" *Art News* (New York) 62, no. 7 (Nov. 1963), p. 62.

PLATE 12

Summer Tools, 1962
Oil, tools, string, metal, glue bottles, and plastic light fixture on three joined canvases
80 x 108 inches
Private collection

During the summer of 1962, Dine executed in rapid succession a number of canvases with tools either affixed to their thickly painted surfaces or dangling from their edges. The *Tool* series, like the *Bathrooms*, alludes to the hardware stores that Dine's family owned in his youth. Unlike bathroom fixtures, tools have become endemic to Dine's practice during the last four decades. Identifying a human trace within their very structures, Dine employs tools as veiled surrogates for his own body and has explained his long-standing veneration as follows: "A tool can be inspiring. Not just because it's some sort of phallic symbol, but because the tool is a beautiful object in itself, it has been refined to be an extension of one's hand, over the centuries, in a process of evolution."[1] Although they relate to his own experiences, the paintings are not as openly personal as Dine's earlier works. Instead, he intended the canvases to provoke individual reactions from each viewer. "I use only new things that are familiar, such as hammers, pliers, etc., so that there will be no confusion about the mystery the viewer brings to the picture,"[2] Dine has explained.

The *Tool* series details the labor of Dine's artistic process. *Summer Tools* bears the hammer, screwdriver, and glue that might have been used in its own construction, while additional elements, such as a light-switch cover and rope, suggest similar paintings that Dine created with quite similar objects. While other canvases from the series juxtapose actual tools with their painted silhouettes to imply action, tools are hung from or attached to the minimally painted surface of *Summer Tool* to suggest a suspension in the creative process. Playing on this suggestion of motion, the barren background of *Summer Tools* functions as a stage set for its elements that seem about to hammer, scrub, or cut their paths across the surface. "I was skirting the issue of painting and making a kind of inanimate theater,"[3] he has said of the *Tool* paintings. Dine has also related this approach to his 1960 *Vaudeville Collage* performance, in which leafy vegetables tossed onto an empty stage appeared to come to life as actors.[4]

Dine has cited the influence of fifteenth-century Flemish painting upon these compositional arrangements, likening his intimate groups of inanimate objects to the Flemish depictions of human subjects within tightly contained pictorial spaces.[5] It has been noted that the formal organization of Dine's *Tool* works from this period anticipate a group of abstract landscapes that the artist would complete in 1963.[6] Indeed, the splashes of color and objects that appear at the top of *Summer Tools* seem to emerge as if figures on a distant horizon, moving into the empty foreground.—KVW

1. Germano Celant and Clare Bell, *Jim Dine: Walking Memory, 1959–1969*, exh. cat. (New York: Guggenheim Museum, 1999), p. 132.

2. Alan Solomon, "Jim Dine and the Psychology of the New Art," *Art International* (Lugano) 8, no. 8 (Oct. 20, 1964), p. 55.

3. Interview with Jim Dine in David Shapiro, in *Jim Dine: Painting What One Is* (New York: Harry N. Abrams, 1981), p. 209.

4. Celant and Bell, *Jim Dine: Walking Memory*, p. 133. For a description of the *Vaudeville Collage* performance, see Julia Blaut, "A 'Painter's Theater': Jim Dine's Environments and Performances," in Celant and Bell, p. 36.

5. Ibid., p. 133.

6. Shapiro, *Jim Dine: Painting What One Is*, p. 31.

Jasper Johns

b. 1930

Jasper Johns was born May 15, 1930, in Augusta, Georgia, and was raised in South Carolina. In the fall of 1947 he enrolled at the University of South Carolina, Columbia, to study art but left in December 1948 to attend the Parsons School of Design, New York, from January to June 1949. Drafted into the United States Army, Johns served from May 1951 to late 1952 in South Carolina, where he operated the Fort Jackson Gallery, exhibiting artworks made by fellow soldiers. After a period of service in Japan, Johns returned to New York, where he met fellow artist Robert Rauschenberg in late 1953.

Regarded as an important bridge between Abstract Expressionism and Pop art and Minimalism, Johns and Rauschenberg worked in close proximity until 1961. Johns was also significantly influenced by his friendships with John Cage and Merce Cunningham (for whom he designed sets and costumes and acted as artistic adviser from 1967 to 1980) and by his admiration for Marcel Duchamp. In late 1954, Johns began to use encaustic to depict flags, targets, maps, numerals, and letters, treating these familiar motifs without recourse to illusionism, and emphasizing the painting's physical presence as an object. In some paintings he incorporated actual three-dimensional forms, such as a ball, a book, or a stretcher.

Johns's first solo exhibition was held at the Leo Castelli Gallery, New York, in January 1958, the success of which firmly established his career. He began to work with Sculp-metal in 1958 and to make cast-bronze sculptures in 1960, when he also started to explore printmaking. His first retrospective was held in 1964 at the Jewish Museum, New York. He continued to develop important motifs in his work, including the map of the United States and the flagstone and crosshatch patterns, which allowed him to explore concepts of literalness, repetition, order, and patterning. In 1972 Johns established a home and studio on the island of Saint Martin. A retrospective organized by the Whitney Museum of American Art traveled, after its New York showing, to Europe, Japan, and San Francisco during 1977 and 1978.

In the 1980s Johns began to explore illusion through the use of trompe l'oeil and the inclusion of "trick" images adopted from perceptual psychology. Recent paintings have addressed the seasons and his own career. Some have included imagistic references to paintings by Paul Cézanne, Matthias Grünewald, and Hans Holbein. A retrospective organized by the Museum of Modern Art, New York, in 1996–97, traveled to Germany and Japan. Johns lives and works in New York, Saint Martin, and Connecticut.

PLATE 2

Flashlight I, 1958
Sculp-metal over flashlight and wood
5¼ x 9⅛ x 3⅞ inches
Sonnabend Collection

From the mid-1950s, Jasper Johns developed a pictorial repertory based on familiar, everyday signs: targets, numbers, and American flags. In his first _Flag_ painting of 1954–55, the edges of the flag coincide exactly with those of the canvas support. By eliminating the traditional figure-ground relationship in painting, Johns muddled the boundaries between real object and art object: _Flag_ functions at once as national symbol, reproduction, and work of art. Such coexistence of object and representation had further implications in a group of small sculptures of lightbulbs and flashlights Johns completed in 1958.

Flashlight I is one of the artist's experiments with Sculp-metal, a substance made from vinyl resin mixed with aluminum powder that can be modeled like clay but hardens into metal. In making the piece, Johns took an actual flashlight and covered it with Sculp-metal, then re-created its surface details by hand. The covering, however, is not complete, and the bulb and glass of the actual flashlight remain visible, essentially standing in for themselves. In making sculptures that both are and are not the thing itself, Johns creates a perceptual conundrum, and, much as Marcel Duchamp's readymades do, raises questions about the status of the art object, the relationship between the handmade and the mass-produced, and what is necessary to distinguish a sculpture from ordinary nonart things. What differentiates Johns's practice from that of Duchamp, whom he greatly admired, is that whereas Duchamp presented his readymades largely as he found them, altering only their position and context, Johns materially transforms his chosen objects. The surface of the flashlight bears the clear marks of physical handling, conveying a strong sense of authorship and manipulation. In accordance with sculptural tradition, Johns positions his form on a base, literally elevating its status from mundane everyday tool to work of art.
—LMcM

PLATE 3

Figure 8, 1959
Encaustic on canvas
20¹/₁₆ x 15 inches
Sonnabend Collection

In 1959, the same year Jasper Johns painted _Figure 8_, he made the following statement: "I am opposed to painting which is concerned with conceptions of simplicity." This declaration might at first seem to be contradicted by this work's "simple" subject matter: a stenciled, painted number eight. But it reveals the acute sensitivity of Johns's approach. Familiar, oft-repeated forms can offer both artist and viewer an interest so profound as to render irrelevant any comparison with allegedly more complex or "original" subjects. By infusing ostensibly plain graphic symbols with intense visual incident and play, Johns's work points to the inadequacy of this conventional opposition.

Encaustic, a mixture of hot beeswax and pigment that was used in ancient Roman frescoes and the American crafts alike, is the pasty medium of _Figure 8_'s extraordinarily worked surface. Dense patches of vibrant Crayola primaries—deep blue, true red, and orange-yellow are interspersed across the curves of the numeral. Underneath the patchy, whitish background lie traces of these same primary colors and a few isolated clippings of matted-down newspaper. Throughout his work with numbers, letters, and other familiar symbols, Johns maintained the appearance of traced stencils and copied-out figures. In _Figure 8_ some of the brushstrokes just outside the eight echo its curves very closely, as if to suggest that the artist had repeatedly traced the figure. At the same time, several white vertical drips appear like frozen brushstrokes—an effect heightened by the use of encaustic, which hardens into a thick,

waxy consistency as it dries. Like that of the Abstract Expressionists who dominated the New York art world when Johns began showing his work in 1958, his painting technique stresses the immediate, material reality of its medium. But the introduction of subject matter and the use of encaustic—a medium that requires meticulous care—distance Johns's work from the spontaneity of the New York School.

Since the beginning of his career, Johns has experimented with generic forms familiar to almost any viewer: flags, maps, numbers, letters, and targets. Instead of representing objects from the world and using painterly devices such as perspective to create the illusion of three-dimensional space, Johns paints symbols and signs directly on the canvas. There is no "original" number eight that served as a model for this painting. Johns thus subtly but irreversibly alters the function of artistic subject matter by using it to encourage us to reconsider precisely those things we thought we already knew, mining the potential richness of a range of familiar, mass-produced visual forms.—RH

PLATE 4

Fool's House, 1962
Oil on canvas with broom, fabric, wood,
and porcelain cup
72 x 36 inches
Collection of Jean Christophe Castelli

Following the success of his first solo exhibition with the Leo Castelli Gallery in 1958, Jasper Johns's painting changed significantly. Actual objects, which were often movable, were increasingly introduced into his work, appropriating the space in front of the canvas and again calling attention to the painting as it exists as both a two- and three-dimensional form. Some critics had labeled Johns's work Neo-Dada, which sparked his interest in, and later friendship with Marcel Duchamp. Both artists were concerned with the visual and intellectual experience of the viewer before a work of art, and, rather than seeking to create an illusion of space, sought to refer to the space actually inhabited by the viewer. More aggressive brushstrokes also began to appear in Johns's work at this time, together with stenciled letters and numbers and a restricted palette including whites, blacks, and grays. The physical characteristics of painting and explicit references to studio practice became central as well, and even provided subject matter and sources of imagery. Overall, a more somber, darker emotional tone prevailed in these works of the early 1960s.

Fool's House shows these developing concerns. The found objects may relate to Duchamp, but here Johns's household items assume an artistic function, becoming studio tools. The broom serves as paintbrush, the towel as paint rag, and the dangling cup as a receptacle for paint. *Fool's House* also evidences Johns's interest in the relations between art, language, and the world; it includes both handwritten labels pointing to the objects included (reinforcing his use of "real" objects rather than the use of trompe l'oeil painting techniques) and the stenciled title of the work itself. The title, however, is split, and would meet up only if the painting were cylindrical in form. This, as well as the presence of a small wood stretcher on the front of the canvas and the cup hanging down, suggests a preoccupation with more complex spatial relations beyond the dimensions of the work itself. The use of elements from the studio and imagery derived from imprinting and smearing—as implied in the traces of the broom's movements—appear elsewhere in Johns's work and indicate the artist's deeper consideration of his process and environment.—LMcM

PLATE 1

Flags, 1987
Encaustic and newspaper on canvas
25½ x 33 inches
Collection of the artist

Jasper Johns began his first flag painting in 1954, after dreaming of painting an American flag. Completely filling the picture plane, Johns's "flag" collapsed the figure-ground relationship, raising questions about the possible coalescence of an object and its representation. Further ambiguities arose about the use of such a politically charged symbol and the artist's intention in employing it at that time, though Johns has stated that a painting of a flag is as much about the physicality of painting as it is about a flag. He also claimed that the use of such familiar imagery as flags, targets, and maps allowed him to work on other levels, and to concentrate on process. Indeed, the original *Flag* (1954–55) shows much experimentation in technique and is rendered in encaustic (pigment suspended in beeswax) over oil paint and collaged newspaper.

The flag became emblematic in Johns' practice, and he has returned to it on many occasions, changing or manipulating the color and rendering its image in various mediums, from graphite to ink and even bronze. In this work dating from 1987, Johns returns to the technique of the original flag painting and to the American flag's true colors, this time doubling the image and orienting the flags vertically rather than horizontally. The flags here, however, are mirror images of the American flag and represent a subtle reordering or manipulation of a by-now familiar emblem in the artist's work.

As with the first *Flag*, the political significance of the gesture of reordering and reassembling such an important national symbol is again ambiguous. In his repeated depictions of this and other familiar cultural signs, Johns in some ways anticipated the concerns of Pop art and signaled a move away from Abstract Expressionism. His consistently painterly treatment of the subject, however, and constant reworking of the flag in a variety of mediums evidence other preoccupations.
—LMcM

Roy Lichtenstein

1923–1997

Roy Lichtenstein was born October 27, 1923, in New York. In 1939 he studied under Reginald Marsh at the Art Students League in New York, and the following year under Hoyt Sherman at the School of Fine Arts at Ohio State University, Columbus. He served in the United States Army from 1943 to 1946, after which he resumed his studies and was hired as an instructor. He obtained an M.F.A. degree in 1949. In 1951 the Carlebach Gallery, New York, organized a solo exhibition of his semiabstract paintings of the Old West. Shortly thereafter, the artist moved to Cleveland, where he continued painting while working as an engineering draftsman to support his growing family.

From 1957 to 1960 Lichtenstein held a teaching position at the New York State College of Education, Oswego. By then he had begun to include loosely drawn cartoon characters in his increasingly abstract canvases. From 1960 to 1963, he lived in New Jersey while teaching at Douglass College, a division of Rutgers University in New Brunswick. He met artists such as Jim Dine, Allan Kaprow, Claes Oldenburg, Lucas Samaras, George Segal, and Robert Whitman, who were experimenting in diverse ways with the interrelationships of art and everyday life. In 1961 he began to make paintings consisting exclusively of comic-strip figures, and introduced his Benday-dot grounds, lettering, and speech balloons; he also started incorporating cropped images from advertisements in his works. From 1964 into the 1970s he successively depicted stylized landscapes and adaptations of paintings by famous artists, geometric elements from Art Deco design (the *Modern* series) and parodies of the Abstract Expressionists' style (the *Brushstroke* series). They all underlined the contradictions of representing three dimensions on a flat surface.

In the early 1970s he explored this formal question further with his abstract *Mirrors* and *Entablatures* series. From 1974 into the 1980s he probed another long-standing issue: the concept of artistic style. All his series of works played with the characteristics of well-known twentieth-century art movements. Lichtenstein continued to question the role of style in consumer culture in his 1990s series of *Interiors*, which included images of his own works as decorative elements.

Since 1962 Lichtenstein's work has been represented by Leo Castelli Gallery, New York. He participated in the Venice Biennale in 1966, and was honored with solo exhibitions in 1967 and 1968 at the Pasadena Art Museum and the Solomon R. Guggenheim Museum, New York, respectively. The artist was the subject of a major retrospective at the Guggenheim in 1994, three years before his death on September 30, 1997.

PLATE 13
Eddie Diptych, 1962

Oil on canvas

Two panels, left: 44 x 16 inches; right: 44 x 35⅞ inches; 44 x 52 inches overall

Sonnabend Collection

Roy Lichtenstein helped usher in the Pop art movement in the United States in the 1960s. Inspired by popular culture and mass media, he made artworks with a new focus on urban culture, exploring the United States and its people in terms of familiar imagery from everyday life. With his large-scale paintings of comic-book panels and his deadpan renditions of advertisements, Lichtenstein celebrated and critiqued some of the more absurd aspects of American society and created a composite portrait of consumerism .

Lichtenstein began making paintings of cartoon characters, comic-strip panels, and generic advertising imagery in 1961. In the same year, he experimented with the diptych format, using it first for paintings based on newspaper and magazine ads. Turning to postwar romance comic books, Lichtenstein culled imagery, plot, and visual elements such as the medium's characteristic speech balloons, expanses of flat color, and extreme close-ups. In *Eddie Diptych*, Lichtenstein isolated the heroine's internal dialogue on one panel, revealing the drama beneath the unemotional stares and clichéd exchange in the scene played out on the larger canvas.

Borrowing conventions associated with commercial printing processes—sharp black outlines, a few bold colors, and Benday dots— Lichtenstein fused fine-art production with the appearance of mass production. The grid of dots that comprises the women's skin in this work mimics the thousands of dots used to create expanses of color by inexpensive printing methods. After experimenting with

making these imitation Benday dots with a brush and a handmade stencil, he switched in 1963 to a manufactured screen that allowed for more precise results.

Yet he recognized the artifice of his task: "I want my art to look programmed or impersonal, but I don't believe I'm being impersonal while I do it."[1] Lichtenstein's painted versions of these scenes are considerably altered from the original sources. He reduced realistic details, simplified narratives, and recomposed the subjects, often combining elements from numerous frames into one, and ultimately achieved in the idealized, iconic look that came to define the most successful of the 1960s comic books. Complicating the idea that Pop elevates mass culture to high art, Lichtenstein's work also underscores the art qualities of the materials of everyday life.—TB

1. Roy Lichtenstein, quoted in Lucy Lippard, *Pop Art*, (New York: Thames and Hudson, 1987), p. 86.

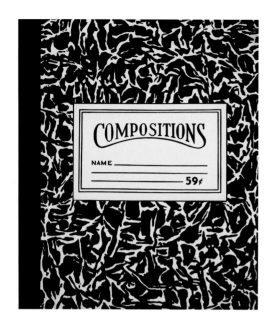

PLATE 14

Compositions II, 1964
Oil on canvas
54 x 47¼ inches
Sonnabend Collection

For many critics who championed Abstract Expressionism in the 1940s and 1950s, the advent of Pop art constituted a violation of the accepted canon of Modernism, which held that true avant-garde art evolved toward a greater and greater degree of abstraction. In its return to representation, Pop's object-centered images appeared regressive. They were considered a throwback to the rigidity of Social Realism of the 1930s rather than a continuation of the utopian ideals ascribed to the emotive abstractions of Jackson Pollock and Mark Rothko. By calling attention to what they considered indifferent transcriptions of found imagery, critics such as Clement Greenberg and Max Kozloff dismissed Pop artists wholesale. In 1962 Kozloff wrote, "Save us from the 'uncharmers,' or permutations thereof, the Rosensteins or the Oldenquists to come!"[1]

For Roy Lichtenstein, the relationship between Pop and abstraction was more complicated than the critics' interpretation. Some works from the early 1960s depict household objects—an electric extension cord or the Roto-Broil electric cooker, for example—culled from newspaper or telephone-book advertisements. In these crude graphics, where details were reduced to dots, dashes, and lines, Lichtenstein found forms connected to Piet Mondrian's grids and Fernand Léger's machine paintings of the 1920s and 1930s.

Lichtenstein painted a series depicting black and white composition notebooks in 1964–65. Unlike his single-object paintings in which the featured item—a jeweled brooch or a golf ball—floats against a patterned or blank background, the *Compositions* canvases are filled edge to edge with their motif. As with Jasper Johns's flags or targets, the notebook and the canvas merge; the painting is seen as object and vice versa, blurring distinctions between representation and abstraction. Lichtenstein's characteristic deadpan humor is evidenced in the parallels between the overall patterning of the marbleized notebook covers and Pollock's allover drip paintings, as well as the blank lines below the title "compositions," which, like so many untitled but numbered Abstract Expressionist compositions, is open-ended and vague.

The critics' idea that abstraction could somehow be pure and unfettered by the real world was undermined by the similarities and analogies Lichtenstein recognized—and even poked fun at—in both abstraction and sources from popular culture. *Compositions II* ultimately takes as its subject the artificiality of artistic representation and questions the role of art in the twentieth century. The wit and strength of Lichtenstein's work lies in its ability to subvert and recontextualize the familiar. By employing nonart images in "high" art places, Lichtenstein challenges us to redefine how we see the world.—TB

1. Max Kozloff, "'Pop' Culture, Metaphysical Disgust, and the New Vulgarians," *Art International* (Lugano) 6, no. 2 (Mar. 1962), p. 36. Reprinted in Christin J. Mamiya, *Pop Art and Consumer Culture: American Super Market* (Austin: University of Texas Press, 1992), p. 156.

PLATE 16

Preparedness, 1968
Oil and Magna on three joined canvases
10 feet x 18 feet
Solomon R. Guggenheim Museum, New York
69.1885.a-.c

In 1963 Roy Lichtenstein defended Pop art against its critics, contending that "there are certain things that are usable, forceful, and vital about commercial art." By choosing comic-book illustrations as a theme, and using simulated Benday dots to suggest cheap printing, Lichtenstein acknowledged (and perhaps questioned) the role of this popular form of entertainment in daily life.

While continuing to use the conventions of comics and advertisements, the artist also cultivated imagery from the history of art. In *Preparedness* he used the Benday-dot technique to make a wall-size painting that suggests the machine paintings of Fernand Léger and the WPA artists of the 1930s, who painted monumental murals, readable at a distance, on themes of workers and everyday life. Lichtenstein followed this practice to an ironic and somewhat subversive end. Painted during a year when public opinion regarding the Vietnam War shifted dramatically, Lichtenstein's massive depiction of machinery and soldiers probes the conventions of selling the promises of the military-industrial complex, while quietly alluding to the naive optimism underlying a call to arms.

Lichtenstein often focused on the way his traditional and mass-media sources resolved the dilemmas of representing three dimensions on a flat picture plane, incorporating their solutions into his own work with witty exaggeration. *Preparedness* plays

the fragmented, Cubist-collage space of Léger against comic-strip modes of suggesting form and the surface quality of objects.

Lichtenstein's inclusion of an airplane window in the third panel of the work foreshadows his engagement with modes of conveying the illusion of reflective glass, which he would explore in a series of paintings of mirrors.
—JB

PLATE 15
Girl with Tear I, 1977
Oil and Magna on canvas
70 x 50 inches
Solomon R. Guggenheim Museum, New York
Gift of the artist, by exchange
80.2732

At first glance, Surrealism would seem to be a subject so remote from Roy Lichtenstein's own formal concerns as to offer him too little to work with. However, Lichtenstein's overview of twentieth-century art and his affinity for historicism propelled him to explore several art movements with which he seemingly had little in common. What attracted him to Surrealism was its orthodoxy; it contained within it, like comic strips or consumer-product ads, the seeds of stereotype, as does any form of art or culture when it is carried to an extreme. Thus Lichtenstein took Surrealism's style and techniques as the subject for a painting series in the 1970s.

His Surrealist-inspired imagery was often based on that of Salvador Dalí, Max Ernst, and particularly René Magritte. Magritte frequently created a trompe-l'oeil world in which a figure or object is pictured in a scale that is at odds with the others in the painting. In most of his canvases, the figures and objects appear as though they could step out of the stage space they inhabit and enter the domain of the spectator. Magritte also took pleasure in the incongruity of metamorphosis, showing a fish being transformed into a woman, a pair of boots into feet. Because of his interests in trompe l'oeil and transformation, Magritte's art was ready-made material for Lichtenstein. In *Girl with Tear I*, he borrows several motifs from Magritte, including an eye similar to that in *The False Mirror* (1928).

Merely to duplicate such works would produce a pastiche of Surrealism; instead Lichtenstein merged prototypical subjects and motifs from one or more Surrealists with pictorial elements from his own oeuvre, creating a new set of images in which the underlying theme is Surrealist. In this painting, he appropriated the image of a melted pocket watch from Dalí's signal painting *The Persistence of Memory* (1931) and transformed it into the "melting" tear that falls from the girl's eye.

Girl with Tear I is one of three related works he made the same year (the others are *Landscape with Figures* and *Female Head*). These works present us with Lichtenstein's interpretation of Surrealism's vocabulary and the deeply recessed space of Giorgio de Chirico or Dalí, while recalling his own paintings of female figures of the early 1960s.
—SRGM

Claes Oldenburg

b. 1929

Claes Oldenburg was born January 28, 1929 in Stockholm. His father was a diplomat, and the family lived in the United States and Norway before settling in Chicago in 1936. Oldenburg studied literature and art history at Yale University, New Haven, from 1946 to 1950. He subsequently studied art under Paul Weighardt at the Art Institute of Chicago from 1950 to 1954. During the first two years of art school, he also worked as an apprentice reporter at the City News Bureau of Chicago. Afterward he opened a studio, where he made magazine illustrations and easel paintings. Oldenburg eventually became an American citizen in December 1953.

In 1957 he moved to New York and met several artists who were doing early performance work, including George Brecht, Allan Kaprow, George Segal, and Robert Whitman. Oldenburg likewise became a prominent figure in Happenings and performance art during the late 1950s and early 1960s. In 1959 the Judson Gallery, New York, exhibited a series of Oldenburg's enigmatic images, ranging from monstrous human figures to everyday objects, made from a mix of drawings, collages, and papier-mâché. In 1961, he opened *The Store*, a re-creation of the environment of the shops in his downtown Manhattan neighborhood. He displayed familiar objects made out of plaster, reflecting American society's celebration of consumption, and was soon heralded as an important Pop artist with critics' recognition of the movement in 1962.

Oldenburg realized his first outdoor public monument in 1967 in the form of a Conceptual performance/action behind the Metropolitan Museum of Art, New York. As a protest against the Vietnam War, he had a crew dig a rectangular hole in the ground the size of a grave and then refill it. Beginning in the mid-1960s he also proposed colossal art projects for several cities, and by 1969 his first such iconic work, *Lipstick (Ascending) on Caterpillar Tracks*, was installed at Yale University. Most of his large-scale projects were made with the collaboration of Coosje van Bruggen, whom he married in 1977. In the mid-1970s and again in the 1990s Oldenburg and van Bruggen collaborated with the architect Frank O. Gehry, eroding the boundaries between architecture and sculpture. In 1991 Oldenburg and van Bruggen executed a binocular-shaped sculpture-building as part of Gehry's Chiat/Day offices in Los Angeles.

Over the past three decades Oldenburg's works have been the focus of numerous performances and exhibitions. In 1985 *Il Corso del Coltello* was performed in Venice, Italy. It included the *Knife Ship I*, a giant Swiss Army knife equipped with oars; for the performance the ship was set afloat in front of the Arsenale in an attempt to combine art, architecture, and theater. *Knife Ship I* traveled to several museums throughout America and Europe from 1986 to 1988. Oldenburg was honored with a solo exhibition of his work at the Museum of Modern Art, New York, in 1969, and with a retrospective organized by the National Gallery of Art, Washington, D.C., and the Solomon R. Guggenheim Museum, New York, in 1995. Oldenburg and van Bruggen live and work in New York City.

PLATE 17

Soft Pay-Telephone, 1963
Vinyl filled with kapok, mounted on painted
wood panel
46½ x 19 x 9 inches
Solomon R. Guggenheim Museum, New York
Gift, Ruth and Philip Zierler in memory of their
dear departed son, William S. Zierler
80.2747

Claes Oldenburg's absorption with the
commonplace was first manifest in his
personal collection of toys, plastic food, and
kitschy knickknacks. These objects served as
prototypes for the pieces the artist included in
his early Happenings and installations. Such
sculptural articles played a more central role
in Oldenburg's fabricated environment *The
Store* (1961), in one version of which he filled
a Manhattan storefront with colorfully painted
simulations of ordinary items—including
articles of clothing (lingerie, in particular) and
sundry food products—which he sold as
merchandise. Because of its conflation of
creativity with commerce, *The Store* is often
cited as a definitive moment in the emergence
of Pop art.

The lumpy wares sold at *The Store*, and their
later incarnations as large-scale, stuffed vinyl
sculptures such as this pay telephone, may be
seen as substitutions for and references to the
human body. Through their malleable forms
and susceptibility to the effects of gravity,
these supple sculptures often suggest specific
anatomical parts: Hamburgers are breasts, a
tube of toothpaste is a phallus. Passive and
limp, but potentially arousable, the pieces

allude to the sexual, a realm that has been
repressed in much Modern, abstract art. By
asserting the sensual through the mundane,
Oldenburg explores the ways in which
everyday objects are so much an extension of
ourselves. Anyone familiar with Sigmund
Freud's interpretation of dreams, in which
domestic items are surrogates for human
anatomy, will find a similar equation in
Oldenburg's art. As the artist has said, "I never
make representations of bodies but of things
that relate to bodies so that the body
sensation is passed along to the spectator
either literally or by suggestion."—NS

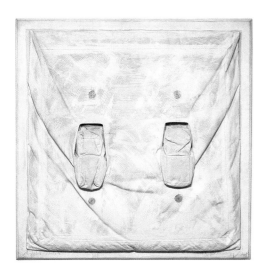

PLATE 18

Soft Light Switches—"Ghost" Version, 1963
Liquitex and graphite on canvas filled with kapok, mounted on canvas over wood
52 x 52 x 9½ inches
The Berardo Collection, Sintra Museum of Modern Art, Portugal

Claes Oldenburg's monumental environmental work *The Store* (1961) was just the beginning of his preoccupation with common, everyday objects and their reconfiguration as artworks. The sculptural items displayed in *The Store*—a wedge of pie, little girls' dresses, a shirt and tie, a pair of sneakers, to name just a few—were generally made from hardened burlap or muslin-coated plaster, often affixed to wire frames and covered with drippy enamel paint. Toward the end of that project, Oldenburg began using softer, more flexible materials to render similar items. These soft works are just that—pliable forms constructed from durable but malleable materials such as canvas or vinyl, stuffed with foam rubber or kapok (silky, natural fibers used as filling for things like sleeping bags). In 1962 Oldenburg exhibited his first three soft works, along with some of the inventory from *The Store*, in an exhibition at the Green Gallery, New York. Their pieces had been cut from patterns of his design and sewn by his wife at that time, Pat Oldenburg. On view were a slice of layer cake, a hamburger, and an ice-cream cone, all rendered on an exaggerated scale and placed directly on the floor.

What Oldenburg was seeking to do with *The Store* was to revive the human element in contemporary urban experience. It is this impulse toward humanizing our environment and the objects that fill it that strongly informs Oldenburg's soft sculptures and other art of the early and mid-1960s. In concentrating on domestic interiors, appliances, and plumbing fixtures, Oldenburg created a group of sculptures of mechanized or electrical items: a typewriter, pay telephone, electrical outlet, and light switches. He made three versions of each in different sizes and forms: hard, soft, and what the artist called a "ghost" version, like this *Light Switch*, which also exists in painted wood and metal as well as supple red vinyl. Oldenburg would often make ghost versions as prototypes for the vinyl works because the seams of the vinyl pieces were too difficult to rip out if they needed to be adjusted and resewn. He came to regard these studies as works in themselves, and considered the white-painted fabric maquettes "more spiritual" incarnations of his soft forms.[1] He would occasionally create the ghost version after executing a work in vinyl.

The industrial products that Oldenburg turned to at this time have nothing soft about them—indeed, sculpture as defined and sanctioned by the Modernist canon is not *supposed* to be soft. It was this profound alteration of sculptural form that so influenced younger artists in the 1960s, such as Eve Hesse. With their skinlike surfaces and undeniably bodily associations, Oldenburg's soft sculptures nudge the latent corporeality of objects into the more ambiguous, but less illusory, realm of real experience.—MD

1. Claes Oldenburg, quoted in Paul Cummings, unpublished interview, Dec. 4, 1973–Jan. 25, 1974, p. 180, on file at the Archives of American Art, Washington, D.C., cited in *Claes Oldenburg: An Anthology*, exh. cat. (New York: Guggenheim Museum), p. 4.

Robert Rauschenberg

b. 1925

Robert Rauschenberg was born Milton Rauschenberg on October 22, 1925, in Port Arthur, Texas. He began to study pharmacology at the University of Texas at Austin before being drafted into the United States Navy, where he served as a neuropsychiatric technician in the Navy Hospital Corps, San Diego. In 1947 he enrolled at the Kansas City Art Institute, and the following year traveled to Paris to study at the Académie Julian.

In the fall of 1948 he returned to the United States to study under Josef Albers at Black Mountain College, near Asheville, North Carolina, which he continued to attend intermittently through 1952. While taking classes at the Art Students League, New York, from 1949 to 1951, Rauschenberg was offered his first solo exhibition at the Betty Parsons Gallery. Among the works he produced in this period are his blueprints, monochromatic white paintings, and black paintings. From fall 1952 to spring 1953 he traveled to Europe and North Africa with Cy Twombly, whom he had met at the Art Students League. During his travels Rauschenberg worked on a series of small collages, hanging assemblages, and small boxes filled with found elements, which he exhibited in Rome and Florence.

Upon his return to New York in 1953 Rauschenberg completed his series of black paintings, using newspaper as the ground, and began to make sculptures created from wood, stones, and other materials found on the streets; paintings with tissue paper, dirt, or gold leaf; and more conceptually oriented works such as *Automobile Tire Print* and *Erased de Kooning Drawing*. By the end of 1953 he had begun his *Red Painting* series of canvases that incorporate newspapers, fabric, and found objects. These evolved in 1954 into the Combines, a term Rauschenberg coined for

his now well-known works that integrated aspects of painting and sculpture and include such objects as a stuffed eagle or goat, street signs, or a quilt and pillow. In late 1953 he met Jasper Johns. The two are considered the most influential artists among those who reacted against Abstract Expressionism in the mid-1950s. Johns and Rauschenberg had neighboring studios, regularly exchanging ideas and discussing their work, until 1961.

Rauschenberg began to silkscreen paintings in 1962. The following year he had his first career retrospective, organized by the Jewish Museum, New York, and was awarded the Grand Prize in Painting at the 1964 Venice Biennale. He spent much of the remainder of the 1960s dedicated to more collaborative projects including printmaking, performance, choreography, set design, and art and technology works. In 1966 he cofounded Experiments in Art and Technology (E.A.T), an organization that sought to promote collaborations between artists and engineers.

In 1970 Rauschenberg established a permanent residence and studio in Captiva, Florida, where he still lives. A retrospective organized by the National Collection of Fine Arts, Washington, D.C., traveled throughout the United States in 1976–78. Rauschenberg himself continued to travel widely, embarking on a number of collaborations with artisans and workshops abroad, which culminated in the Rauschenberg Overseas Culture Interchange (ROCI) project from 1985 to 1991. In 1997–98 the Solomon R. Guggenheim Museum, New York, and Guggenheim Museum Soho exhibited the largest retrospective of Rauschenberg's work to date, which traveled to Houston and Europe in 1998–99.

PLATE 5

Canyon, 1959
Combine painting: oil, pencil, paper, fabric, metal, cardboard box, printed paper, printed reproductions, photograph, wood, paint tube, and mirror on canvas, with oil on bald eagle, string, and pillow
81¾ x 70 x 24 inches
Sonnabend Collection

Robert Rauschenberg's celebrated Combines, begun in the mid-1950s, fused two-dimensional painting and three-dimensional sculpture. These works brought real-world images and objects into the realm of abstract painting and subverted sanctioned divisions between painting and sculpture. Realized in essentially two formats—as Combine paintings, like *Canyon*, and freestanding Combines—this seminal body of work would occupy the artist until 1962, when he returned to two-dimensional painting with the introduction of the silkscreen process. The full range of Rauschenberg's artistic vocabulary—a sense of temporality; the use of grid formats; doublings, mirrorings, and reversals; and a feel for human scale—appears throughout the Combines.

The central element of *Canyon* is a taxidermic bald eagle presented to Rauschenberg by his friend, fellow artist Sari Dienes, who lived and worked in the studios above Carnegie Hall in Manhattan. Found in the garbage outside her building, this emblem of American freedom had belonged to one of her neighbors, a former member of Teddy Roosevelt's Rough Riders. The startling inclusion of three-dimensional animal forms in the Combines first occurred in an untitled work from 1954; this unique approach to the manipulation of the picture plane reached its apogee with *Canyon* and *Monogram* (1955–59).

As Rauschenberg was at work on *Canyon*, he became preoccupied with a series of solvent transfer drawings (a process invented by him) based on the thirty-four cantos of Dante's *Inferno*, a project that would take him two and a half years to complete. His interest in late medieval literature was coupled at this time with an awareness of Greek mythology, which found expression in a loosely grouped series of Combines: *Three Traps for Medea*, *Gift for Apollo*, *Pail for Ganymede*, and *Canyon* (all 1959).

Canyon references the episode in Greek mythology in which Zeus, in the form of an eagle, offers Ganymede, a youth of great beauty, to the gods as a cup bearer. In the Combine painting, the bald eagle, covered in black paint, perches on a cardboard box that in turn is balanced on a piece of wood suggesting a branch, from which hangs a pillow. Above the eagle's head is an assortment of cut and torn commercial graphics and newspaper clippings. Various photographic reproductions, many in the form of postcards or images cut from contemporary magazines, depict the Statue of Liberty and the night sky with Jupiter clearly visible. These, as well as the applied elements, including a tin can, quote Ganymede's legend. As is typical of his Combines, Rauschenberg here incorporated personal elements, such as the photograph taken by the artist of his infant son Christopher reaching upward and the vintage photograph of his parents' car (modes of transportation are common themes in Rauschenberg's work). Some critics have interpreted this Combine as a veiled coding of homoerotism. The artist has decidedly rejected this reading.—SD

PLATE 6

Dylaby, 1962

Combine painting: oil, wood, and metal on canvas tarpaulin

9 feet 1½ inches x 7 feet 3 inches x 1 foot 3 inches

Sonnabend Collection

Dubbed Combines by their creator, the large-scale assemblages that Robert Rauschenberg began making in 1954 are among his most celebrated works. *Bed* (1955) features dramatic, gestural drips of paint across a patchwork quilt nailed to a stretcher. *Monogram* (1955–59) includes a taxidermic Angora goat wearing a rubber tire around its middle. These works grew out of the incorporation of collage elements into Rauschenberg's otherwise abstract *Red Paintings* of 1953–54 and out of his intense dialogue with composer John Cage, choreographer Merce Cunningham, and fellow painter Jasper Johns. They testify to his exuberant embrace of all manner of raw material—as well as his sensitive dedication to the principles of formal composition.

In *Dylaby* Rauschenberg begins with a large canvas tarp, half of which is attached to the wall and the other half left to drape in folds reaching the ground. A skateboard, a rusty Coca-Cola sign, and other tacked-up fragments create a spare, almost classically balanced composition. Rauschenberg's recurring use of the color red imbues the work with a visual narrative, one that climaxes with a splotch of red paint outlined with black crayon as if for emphasis. The lines of dripping red that escape this outline suggest a tension between design and artlessness, control and chance. Rauschenberg's handling of color also sets up a dialogue between the artist's painted marks and the work's ready-made components. In *Dylaby* the red, yellow, and white lettering of the Coca-Cola sign is echoed in two disks—one red, one yellow—set next to a large rectangular swatch of white paint. (In another nod to the self-conscious artistry underlying what at first appears a random configuration, a smaller blue disk above them invokes the familiar framework of the primary colors.) Two round stains in the lower center of the tarp echo the shapes of the red and yellow disks, so that one system of mimicry and repetition doubles another. Yet despite these precise compositional devices, *Dylaby* has a spontaneous, almost slapdash feel. Its striking heterogeneity is indeed the work's defining feature.

Dylaby is one component from a larger installation Rauschenberg created for an exhibition of the same name held in 1962 at the Stedelijk Museum, Amsterdam; its title is an amalgamation of the two Dutch words *dynamisch* and *labyrint*. The curators asked the artists (Niki de Saint Phalle, Daniel Spoerri, and Jean Tinguely, among others), to collaborate on a single sculptural environment: a labyrinth to walk through. This proved too complicated, and each artist completed a separate project. For his part, Rauschenberg created a streetscape with rectangular forms enclosed by wire fences that contained assemblages of found objects: an airplane wing, seashells, clocks operating at different speeds and times, and the signage, tarp, and other items from this tableaux. Metamorphosed from junkyard relic to poetic art object, *Dylaby* retains something of its decrepit origins.—RH

PLATE 7

Barge, 1962–63

Oil and silkscreened ink on canvas

6 feet 7⅞ inches x 32 feet 2 inches

Solomon R. Guggenheim Museum, New York, and Guggenheim Museum Bilbao, with additional funds contributed by Thomas H. Lee and Ann Tenenbaum; the International Director's Council and Executive Committee Members; and funds from additional donors: Ulla Dreyfus-Best, Norma and Joseph Saul Philanthropic Fund, Elizabeth Rea, Eli Broad, Dakis Joannou, Peter Norton, Peter Lawson-Johnston, Michael Wettach, Peter Littmann, Tiqui Atencio, Bruce and Janet Karatz, and Giulia Ghirardi Pagliai

97.4566

In 1962 Rauschenberg first used commercially produced silkscreens to make large-format paintings based on his own photographs and found media images. These paintings may be considered an extension of the transfer drawings he executed between 1958 and 1962, in which he directly transferred the contents of newspapers and magazines, including ads, images, maps, and comics, onto sheets of paper. Since he could photographically enlarge imagery onto the silkscreens, this process freed him from the scale restrictions of the transfer technique and allowed him to easily reuse images in varied contexts. As Rauschenberg wrote in a text within his artwork *Autobiography* (1968), he "began silk screen paintings to escape familiarity of objects and collage" that populated his Combines.

Barge, comprised of a single canvas measuring more than thirty feet in width, is the largest of his silkscreened paintings. This monumental work in black, white, and gray incorporates many of the motifs that Rauschenberg used again and again in his seventy-nine silkscreen paintings: the urban environment (water towers on a rooftop), athletes and men of action (swimmers, football players, and firemen), space exploration and flight (a satellite, a rocket, radar dishes, mosquitoes, and birds), modes of transportation (a truck), and examples from art history (Diego Velázquez's *Venus and Cupid*, known as the "Rokeby Venus"). The square format of the screens provides a gridlike structure for the composition, which is further embellished by areas of gestural paint application.

Rauschenberg sought to highlight his process by emphasizing the edges of the silkscreens and the individual swipes of the squeegee used to apply the ink. As in his earlier Combines, elements are layered in an exploration of depth and perspective. On the left edge of the canvas, the difference between pictorial and photographic illusions of depth is illustrated by a clearly rendered isometric box floating beneath a rectangle of gestural strokes that reinforces the flat picture plane. An image of a headlight leads toward a mosquito, which guides the viewer into the body of the painting, a composition of repetitive forms (the pinwheel shape of the mosquito is mimicked by the photographer's strobe-light shield, the satellite, and the radar dishes) and narrative vignettes (the umbrella-like strobe-light shield seems to prevent a deluge of dripping paint from hitting the football players below).—JY

PLATE 8

Untitled, 1963
Oil, silkscreened ink, metal, and plastic
on canvas
82 x 48 x 6¼ inches
Solomon R. Guggenheim Museum, New York
Purchased with funds contributed by Elaine
and Werner Dannheisser and The Dannheisser
Foundation
82.2912

Robert Rauschenberg first explored the new medium of silkscreen in black and white (as in _Barge_, p. 109), but by summer 1963 he had introduced color. The paintings of that period, including _Untitled_, best demonstrate the ways in which the artist exploited the imperfections of the silkscreen process, subverting a perfect registration by not aligning the screens or by not using all of the colors in four-color printing (blue, red, yellow, and black). The gestural application of pigment in certain areas and the addition of found materials (a technique reminiscent of his earlier Combines), like the metal and plastic objects in _Untitled_, assert the handmade, as opposed to mechanical nature of the paintings. The silkscreens capture the random and unending visual stimulation that one encounters in daily life, as well as the unavoidable barrage of visual imagery produced by the mass media. Rauschenberg also frequently includes personal references. In _Untitled_ the dancer Merce Cunningham—with whom he has collaborated on theater and costume design since 1954 and with whose company he had toured Europe in summer 1963—is the central image, turned to lie on its side.

The use of recognizable popular imagery and the application of a commercial technique led critics to identify Rauschenberg with other artists working in this idiom, including Andy Warhol, who also began to use the silkscreen process in his work at about the same time. Although Rauschenberg is certainly of great significance to Pop art for his use of found commercial imagery, repetition of images, and his thwarting of distinctions between high and low art, his paintings of the 1960s tended to be less depersonalized and more metaphoric than Pop.

Rauschenberg was awarded the International Grand Prize in Painting at the Venice Biennale in 1964 for his exhibition of Combines and silkscreen paintings. Thereafter, he destroyed the screens used for those works so as to clear the slate for his next artistic endeavors. He concentrated for the remainder of the decade on performance and technology-based artworks; some critics have noted that his disdain for a fixed point of view and his need for simultaneity and materiality were well served by performance art. Transfer techniques, though, including silkscreening, continue to be an important method for Rauschenberg to incorporate photographic imagery in his works.—JY

James Rosenquist

b. 1933

James Rosenquist was born November 29, 1933, in Grand Forks, North Dakota. He took classes at the Minneapolis School of Art in 1948. Between 1952 and 1954 he learned traditional painting techniques from Cameron Booth at the University of Minnesota, Minneapolis, and worked as a commercial painter during the summer. In 1955 he moved to New York and enrolled at the Art Students League. In New York, he met Robert Indiana, Jasper Johns, Ellsworth Kelly, and Robert Rauschenberg, among others. During this period he worked on small-format, abstract paintings. From 1957 to 1960 he supported himself by painting billboards, becoming completely conversant with the techniques of enlarging photographic images on a colossal scale. He subsequently began to incorporate fragmented images from advertising, movies, and commercial art into his works.

Held in 1962 at the Green Gallery, New York, his first solo show received much attention from the public and the press. Rosenquist stirred viewers' awareness of their relation to mass media, with works characterized by huge scale, hyperrealism, and popular imagery painted in either bright colors or muted grays. Since 1962 his work has been systematically included in exhibitions of Pop art.

In 1964 he joined the stable of Leo Castelli Gallery, New York, and Galerie Ileana Sonnabend began to show his work in Paris. In 1968 the artist produced his first "environment paintings," images of enlarged fragments of unrelated everyday objects. The artist experimented with sculpture, cinema, and lithography in the early 1970s. In 1976 he moved to Aripeka, Florida. Shown at the 1978 Venice Biennale, his painting *F-111* (1964–65), which covered four walls of a room in the international pavilion, depicted historical symbols, signs of affluence, and enlarged

details of military hardware, addressing American war propaganda. In the late 1970s and 1980s Rosenquist made images of women juxtaposed with a machine aesthetic in dynamic, layered compositions.

The Whitney Museum of American Art, New York, organized Rosenquist's first important museum show in 1972. The artist was also honored by several comprehensive exhibitions in the 1980s. A retrospective of his paintings took place in 1991 at the IVAM Centre Julio González, Valencia, Spain. The University Art Museum, California State University, Long Beach, mounted a traveling show of his complete graphic work in 1993. In March 1998 the Deutsche Guggenheim Berlin unveiled *The Swimmer in the Econo-mist* (1997–98), the museum's first site-specific commissioned painting. A major retrospective of Rosenquist's work, organized by the Solomon R. Guggenheim Museum, New York, is forthcoming in 2003–04. Rosenquist lives and works in New York and Aripeka.

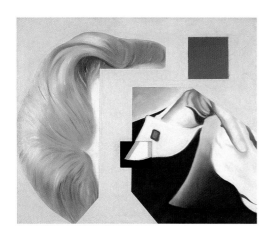

PLATE 19

Balcony, 1961
Oil on canvas and Plexiglas, with mirror
5 feet x 6 feet 1 inch
Sonnabend Collection

Balcony, from 1961, is one of James Rosenquist's first works to contain materials not traditionally found in painting. It features a square mirror near the upper right-hand corner and a rectangular piece of Plexiglas in the center of the image. Starting in 1962–63, tin, clear plastic, aluminum, wood, and mirrored glass began to appear regularly in Rosenquist's almost mural-size paintings. These additions are in many ways comparable to Jasper Johns's and Robert Rauschenberg's experimentation with newsprint, fabric, and other materials from daily life. Rosenquist's use of recognizable subjects culled from mass culture also aligns him with other Pop artists. But the vast scale, cinematic feel, and distinctly suburban iconography of Rosenquist's painting set it stylistically apart from the work of his contemporaries.

In the shellacked curves of a woman's golden bouffant hairdo and the debonair flash of a man's cufflink—the two motifs that seem about to fit together like pieces of a puzzle in the center of _Balcony_—a clichéd story of dry martinis, manicured lawns, and backyard swimming pools seems about to click into vivid motion. The flat, anonymous feel of Rosenquist's painting technique has an overtly commercial look, one that is often attributed to his training as a sign painter. But employed in massive paintings, this technique endows larger-than-life forms with a surreal, three-dimensional plasticity. Rosenquist heightens this otherworldly effect by using a white-lead base mixed with his colors, which gives them a filtered, almost Technicolor appearance. Finally he fragments and juxtaposes the

objects in his paintings so that the apparently arbitrary combinations seem to follow an idiosyncratic, dreamlike logic.

In _Balcony_ the vacuity of Rosenquist's iconography—a panorama of the suburban banal—echoes in the void that is signified by the mirror in the corner. Depending on one's physical position, the mirror may also reflect the viewer's gaze, interrupting the act of viewing with a reminder of that act itself. For inside Rosenquist's massively scaled work are shards of an intimate, perhaps clandestine encounter, which also inevitably brings to mind scenes from movies and television. His painting thus suggests that in contemporary life the most public and private spaces of perception can never be completely separated. In _Balcony_ widely recognizable subject matter is closely coupled with the private challenge of contemplating Rosenquist's vast and cryptic image.—RH

PLATE 20

Coenties Slip Studio, 1961
Oil on shaped canvas
34 x 43 inches
Collection of the artist

Painted in the artist's Lower Manhattan studio during a winter snowstorm in 1961, *Coenties Slip Studio* is a mise-en-scène of James Rosenquist's studio environment that captures a particular visual impression yet also conveys his observations, emotions, and desires during the storm. Fitting together like pieces of a puzzle, the foreground motifs of an egg, fork, and spoon connote the artist's hunger during the storm, while his loneliness and isolation are expressed in the fantasy of a "platinum-blond" companion rendered as the length of hair articulating the right side of the canvas. The gray, shadowy background forms suggest the snow-covered cars in the streets outside the artist's window. Rosenquist's studio is reflected in the concave surface of the spoon, while the bright-yellow yoke of a fried egg brightens the interior on a cold, dark day, as the artist put it, "like an orange in a fried-fish shop."[1] The interplay between the colorful egg and dining utensils superimposed on the grisaille background articulates the three domains of the painting: the studio interior; the snowy, exterior world; and the fantasy realm signified by the woman's hair. That the motif of the platinum blond was painted on a separate piece of shaped canvas, appended to the right side of the otherwise traditionally shaped rectangular format, heightens the sense of disconnection between fantasy and real world.

The painting's small format—about two and a half by three feet—reflects its personal, intimate nature. *Coenties Slip Studio* directly and powerfully asserts Rosenquist's dictum, "All my paintings are autobiographical."[2] It exemplifies the visually enigmatic narratives he was experimenting with in the early 1960s, which were also efforts to capture prosaic events, thoughts, and actions in abstracted compositions of collagelike imagery.—SB

1. James Rosenquist, in conversation with the author, March 2003.

2. Ibid.

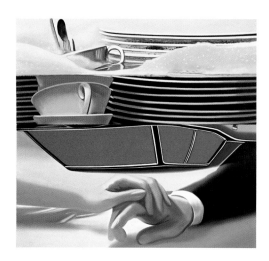

PLATE 21

The Facet, 1978

Oil on canvas

7 feet 6 inches x 8 feet

Lilja Art Fund Foundation, Basel,

On deposit to Musée d'Art Moderne et

d'Art Contemporain, Nice

The Facet is an example of James Rosenquist's remarkable ability to elucidate the goals and expectations of American consumer society through the material goods it so highly values. Rosenquist's tripartite composition conflates the expectations of partnership and security with commercial objects and the concrete world with private concerns and emotions. Layered images of soapy, unwashed dishes, an overturned car, and the touching hands of a couple appear at once dissonant and narrative. The overturned car is the key to the painting's meaning, as the glowing red windows also articulate the ruby of an engagement ring—a visual pun that connects the literal "facets" of the gem and the metaphoric "facets" of the woman's traditional role, represented by the dishes above, to the man's hand supporting hers. Rosenquist's picture seems to articulate, with some irony, the conventional opportunities for women; in the words of the artist, "The promise of an engagement ring is a new car and dirty dishes."[1] The work contemplates the exchange value of the relationship between husband and wife and the promise of that partnership. The progression of cropped, snapshotlike images stacked one on top of another—from couple to car and ring to dirty dishes—pits the banality of actual day-to-day existence against the flimsy logic of society's heightened, often unrealistic, expectations for happiness.

As is often the case with Rosenquist's works, meaning is distilled through visual synecdoches and symbolism: The hands summarize the couple and their partnership; dishes represent the quotidian realities of domesticity; the automobile signifies convenience, material wealth, and security. The obvious salaciousness and forwardness of each image is eye-catching—proffered in the slick manner of advertising—but the combination elides all commercial reasoning and suggests a more subtle investigation. Realized expectations and fulfilled desires rise no further than a pile of dirty dishes. Seemingly enigmatic, upon further contemplation the images in _The Facet_ form a cohesive narrative in which disparate objects are combined in a resonant commentary.—SB

1. James Rosenquist, in conversation with the author, March 2003.

PLATE 22

The Meteor Hits the Swimmer's Pillow, 1997
Oil on linen, with metal bedsprings
8 feet x 5 feet 9 inches
Courtesy Bernard Jacobson Gallery, London

For much of his career James Rosenquist's work has registered a fascination with space and scientific phenomena. Some of his paintings document the United States space program, and one series addresses the theory of relativity and speed of light. And in a group of four works that includes *The Meteor Hits the Swimmer's Pillow*, Rosenquist utilizes a memory of a meteor falling to earth. He recollects that during his childhood, in 1938, a meteor crashed through the roof of a neighbor woman's house in Minnesota, injuring her hip as she was lying in bed. In *The Meteor Hits Brancusi's Pillow* (1997–99) Rosenquist parlays the memory into the canon of art history. Before striking the artist's pillow, the meteor mingles with Brancusi's sculptures. In *The Meteor Hits Picasso's Bed* (1996–99) it hovers larger than life, fixed in the background like a massive glowing peril, and in *The Meteor Hits Monet's Garden* (1999), it falls out of the sky into a peaceful oasis.

First referenced in Rosenquist's three-painting suite *The Swimmer in the Econo-mist* (1997–98), the "Swimmer" is a symbolic reference to the artist. As Rosenquist explained, "There's an old Venetian saying, 'The artist swims in the water, the critic stands ashore.' So the swimmer is the active party. And the economy is a dream."[1] In *The Meteor Hits the Swimmer's Pillow*, the celestial rock hurtles into the pillow situated on a bed that is accented by real metal bedsprings attached to the surface of the canvas. The bright pink bed frame is situated against a dynamic vortex of color and fragmented, brand-name detergent logos. Rosenquist did not employ the meteor

in these works as an obvious metaphor for the source of creative inspiration for the referenced artists, but rather as a meditation on day-to-day questions of existence and the unexpected events that drastically change the course of one's life. Rosenquist emphasizes that life's unexpected events are perfectly democratic, discriminating neither the rich nor serving the purposes of the vox populi: "Good old mother nature doesn't qualify."[2]—SB

1. Robert Rosenblum, "Interview with James Rosenquist," in *James Rosenquist: The Swimmer in the Econo-mist*, exh. cat. (New York: Guggenheim Museum, 1998), p. 10.

2. James Rosenquist, in conversation with the author, March 2003.

Andy Warhol

1928–1987

Andy Warhol was born Andrew Warhola on August 6, 1928, in Pittsburgh. He received his B.F.A. from the Carnegie Institute of Technology, Pittsburgh, in 1949. That same year he came to New York, where he soon became successful as a commercial artist and illustrator. During the 1950s Warhol's drawings were published in *Glamour* and other magazines and displayed in department stores; he became known for his illustrations of I. Miller shoes. In 1952 the Hugo Gallery in New York presented a show of Warhol's illustrations for stories by Truman Capote. Warhol traveled in Europe and Asia in 1956.

By the early 1960s Warhol began to paint comic-strip characters and images derived from advertisements; this work was characterized by the repetition of images of common subjects such as Coca-Cola bottles and Campbell's Soup cans. Warhol's silkscreened "commodities" were exhibited for the first time in 1962, initially at the Ferus Gallery, Los Angeles, then in a solo exhibition at the Stable Gallery, New York. By 1963 he had substituted the silkscreen process for hand painting. Working with assistants, he produced series of disaster scenes, flowers, and celebrity portraits, as well as three-dimensional facsimile Brillo boxes and cartons of other well-known household products.

Starting in the mid-1960s at The Factory, his New York studio, Warhol concentrated on making films that were marked by repetition and an emphasis on boredom. In the 1970s he produced monumental portraits of Mao Tse-tung, commissioned portraits, and the *Hammer and Sickle* series (1977). Warhol also became interested in writing: with his staff at The Factory, he began to publish *Interview* magazine in 1969, and his *The Philosophy of Andy Warhol (from A to B and Back Again)* was published in 1975. A major retrospective of Warhol's work organized by the Pasadena Art Museum in 1970 traveled in the United States and abroad. In 1989 the Museum of Modern Art, New York, mounted another important retrospective. Inaugurated in 1994, the Andy Warhol Museum in Pittsburgh continuously exhibits paintings, sculpture, and films by the artist and houses an important collection of related documents, ephemera, and source material. Warhol died February 22, 1987, in New York.

PLATE 24
Flowers, 1964
Silkscreened ink on canvas
81 x 81 inches
Sonnabend Collection

In 1964, Andy Warhol had his first exhibition at the Leo Castelli Gallery in New York and presented his new series *Flowers*. Showing with Castelli had been a goal of his for some time. By this year, Warhol had already made a name for himself with his Campbell's Soup cans, disaster pictures, and celebrity portraits, and his status in the avant-garde was secure. In reviewing the Castelli show, David Bourdon described the *Flowers* as "cutout gouaches by Matisse set adrift on Monet's lily pond."[1] Not all critics would have agreed with such lofty high-art analogies; Warhol himself likened the *Flowers* to "cheap awnings,"[2] and this reference to a mass-produced product is not so far from the reality of their making. Using silkscreens to apply ink to canvas (already his preferred method for several years), Warhol had taken the industrial implications of that commercial technique to a logical extreme by turning his studio into an assembly line of sorts. The Factory, as his loft on Forty-seventh Street was known, was the artist's studio as well as a social scene, and Warhol enlisted friends and assistants to help churn out silkscreen works en masse, including the many *Flowers* paintings.

While the same image is used repeatedly in all the *Flowers* canvases (Warhol found the original in a women's magazine; it had won second prize in a snapshot contest),[3] each differs in color, size, or orientation. Some are as large as nine feet square, and others measure only five by five inches. Works of varied dimensions were meant to be installed together in a single space in order to create the sense that one is looking at wallpaper or a film. He would fully articulate this impulse soon after in his *Cow* wallpaper, which covered the walls of Castelli's gallery in 1966, and in the countless hours of his many films. After a large group of *Flowers* was shown in 1965 at Ileana Sonnabend's gallery in Paris, Warhol declared that he would devote himself to film and no longer make paintings. This retirement announcement immediately proved to be premature and a bit disingenuous, as his Factory did not cease painting production or concentrate solely on filmmaking, though Warhol was quite occupied with that medium for the next several years.—MD

1. David Bourdon, "Andy Warhol," *The Village Voice*, Dec. 3, 1964, as quoted in Rainer Crone, *Andy Warhol* (New York: Praeger, 1970), p. 30.

2. Ibid.

3. Ibid.

PLATE 25

Early Colored Liz (Chartreuse), 1963
Silkscreened ink on canvas
40 x 40 inches
Sonnabend Collection

PLATE 26

Early Colored Liz (Turquoise), 1963
Silkscreened ink on canvas
40 x 40 inches
Sonnabend Collection

Elizabeth Taylor's demure gaze stares out from Andy Warhol's two silkscreen paintings from 1963: *Early Colored Liz (Chartreuse)* and *Early Colored Liz (Turquoise)*. If intimations of mortality seem to have seeped into the stagy lifelessness of Taylor's lipsticked grin, it is not accidental. Warhol began painting Taylor when she was critically ill, just as he first painted Marilyn Monroe after her suicide and Jackie Kennedy after her husband's assassination. It would seem that in Warhol's pantheon, beauty must be magnificently doomed. While he would make silkscreens that contained multiple images of these iconic women, in 1963–64 Warhol made close-up "portraits" that isolated their individual faces against brightly colored backgrounds, adding color to their eyes and lips like a makeup artist.

Warhol depicted Taylor many times, often alluding to the romantic or tragic episodes in her dramatic life. In a 1962 silkscreen he used a photograph of Taylor accompanied by two of the famous men in her life—husband Mike Todd and Eddie Fisher—along with Fisher's then-wife Debbie Reynolds, who was notoriously ousted by Taylor after Todd's death in a plane crash in 1958. Warhol depicted Taylor in many guises: as an innocent eleven-year-old in *National Velvet*, as a gorgeous star in studio publicity stills, and in elaborate costume for *Cleopatra*, the very expensive box-office failure for which Taylor received an unprecedented one million dollars. That viewers would already know well the many public scandals Taylor courted and endured motivated Warhol's selection of her as the perfect, ready-made, tragically glamorous subject.

The tension between an implied yet unknowable interior and a masklike public persona marks all of Warhol's celebrity portraits, begun—along with his use of the photo-silkscreen, originally a commercial technique—in 1962. Revealing the original newsprint image as an enlarged map of tiny dots, silkscreen functions as a photograph of a photograph, registering the artificiality of the original image in its new incarnation. Transformed by closely cropped compositions and bright washes of color, Warhol's silkscreens vividly illustrate both sides of America's fascination with celebrity: its vision of the star is simultaneously sentimental and garish, sensual and wholesome, intimate and untouchable.—RH

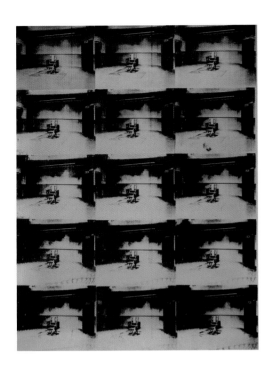

PLATE 27

Orange Disaster #5, 1963
Acrylic and silkscreen enamel on canvas
8 feet 10 inches x 6 feet 9½ inches
Solomon R. Guggenheim Museum, New York
Gift, Harry N. Abrams Family Collection
74.2118

Andy Warhol announced his disengagement from the process of aesthetic creation in 1963: "I think somebody should be able to do all my paintings for me," he told art critic Gene Swenson.[1] The Abstract Expressionists had seen the artist as a heroic figure, alone capable of imparting his poetic vision of the world through gestural abstraction. Warhol, like other Pop artists, used found printed images from newspapers, publicity stills, and advertisements as his subject matter; he adopted silkscreening, a technique of mass reproduction, as his medium. And, unlike the Abstract Expressionists, who searched for a spiritual pinnacle in their art, Warhol aligned himself with the signs of contemporary mass culture. His embrace of subjects traditionally considered debased—from celebrity worship to food labels—has been interpreted both as an exuberant affirmation of American culture and as a thoughtless espousal of the "low." The artist's perpetual examination of themes of death and disaster suggests yet another dimension to his art.

Warhol was preoccupied with news reports of violent death—suicides, car crashes, assassinations, and executions. In the early 1960s he began to make paintings, such as *Orange Disaster #5*, with the serial application of images revolving around the theme of death. "When you see a gruesome picture over and over again," he commented, "it doesn't really have any effect." Yet *Orange Disaster #5*, with its electric chair repeated fifteen times, belies this statement. Warhol's painting speaks to the constant reiteration of tragedy in the media, and becomes, perhaps, an attempt to exorcise this image of death through repetition. However, it also emphasizes the pathos of the empty chair waiting for its next victim, the jarring orange only accentuating the horror of the isolated seat in a room with a sign blaring SILENCE.

Warhol's death and disaster pictures underscore the importance of the vanitas theme—that death will take us all—in his oeuvre. His vanitas imagery has a particularly American cast: he recorded American disasters, the consumption of American products (including movie stars), and, as art historian Sidra Stich has pointed out, American modes of death, such as execution by electrocution.—JB

1. Gene Swenson, "What Is Pop Art?" *Art News* (New York) 62, no. 7 (Nov. 1963), p. 144.

PLATE 23

Four Colored Campbell's Soup Cans, 1965
Acrylic and silkscreened ink on four
framed canvases
36¼ x 24 inches each
Sonnabend Collection

Warhol first exhibited a series of thirty-two paintings depicting Campbell's Soup cans in 1962 at the Ferus Gallery in Los Angeles. Gallerist Irving Blum installed them on a shelf mounted to the wall, stressing a gallery-as-supermarket correlation that caused some initial hostile response. A neighboring gallery, for example, placed rows of the actual soup cans in their window in protest, selling them for the market value of twenty-nine cents.

By 1965, the year that these *Four Colored Campbell's Soup Cans* were produced, Warhol, who had enjoyed success as a commercial artist in New York in the 1950s, was well established in the art world and was employing assistants to help in the production of his work in his studio, The Factory. In his now famous exhibition at New York's Stable Gallery in 1964, visitors made their way past stacks of piled up wooden boxes that he had had silkscreened on all sides to look like boxes of Brillo pads, Mott's Apple Juice, and Heinz Tomato Ketchup. "Shoppers" walked among the aisles of piled-up "products" as if in a crowded warehouse and could carry away their purchases in clear plastic bags. While re-creating actual consumer items and selling them as art represented a step beyond the depiction of soup-can labels in his paintings, Warhol later returned to the motif, which in essence became a kind of brand or logo for the artist himself and his practice in general.

The first *Soup Cans* incorporated a combination of processes, including hand painting, but the replication of the labels soon came to be streamlined, using just a silkscreen technique. *Four Colored Campbell's Soup Cans* shows more complex layering and repetition as well as the brighter colors that characterize Warhol's later work in this medium. The removal of traces of the artist's hand and the assembly-line nature of his production suggest the artist as a machine, which was a preoccupation of Warhol's at the time. "The reason I am painting this way," he famously said, "is that I want to be a machine, and I feel that whatever I do and do machinelike is what I want to do."

Warhol's strategy of appropriation and his use of common middle-class commodities followed a tradition already present in Modern art (from Marcel Duchamp's readymades, for example, to Jasper Johns's sculpture of the late 1950s). But his serial replication of images further questioned the idea of the work of art as the unique expression of an individual, and his use of the most ordinary, readily available consumer products can be seen as a critique of the banality and anonymity of modern life.—LMcM

PLATE 28

One Hundred and Fifty Multicolored Marilyns,
1979
Acrylic and silkscreen enamel on canvas
6 feet 6 inches x 34 feet 6 inches
Guggenheim Museum Bilbao
1997.19

The late 1970s and early 1980s signaled an elaboration of Andy Warhol's visual language, where he revisited some themes and developed new ones. Stylistically his work evolved into more intricate painterly virtuosity and included new kinds of spatial layering, forceful hues, and overlapping images, which infinitely complicated the repetition of his earlier silkscreens. A mood of personal and public retrospection pervades many of these late works.

The image of Marilyn Monroe first appeared in Warhol's work in 1962, the year of Monroe's death. In *Gold Marilyn*, an image of the star's face is set against a gold background to deliberately emulate the quality of a religious icon. In 1962 alone Warhol made numerous silkscreens using the same iconic photo reproduction of Monroe, with her lips parted and eyes seductive and heavy-lidded, in different configurations: two Marilyns, four, six, then twenty-five, a tondo, and a diptych. The quantity of repetition in *One Hundred and Fifty Multicolored Marilyns* expresses most clearly the potentially unlimited replication of this—or any—image.

During the 1970s Warhol created portraits of friends such as Liza Minnelli and Mick Jagger, as well as a series devoted to Chinese leader Mao Tse-tung, and began publishing *Interview* in 1969, a magazine devoted initially to film and ultimately to covering entertainers, the fashionable, and the famous. *One Hundred and Fifty Multicolored Marilyns* is part of a continuum of Warhol's well-documented obsession with fame, but it is also a nostalgic return to his first celebrity subject. In fact, this work is one of two unusually large and wide paintings of 1979 of two extraordinarily famous women, Monroe and Mona Lisa (as painted by Leonardo da Vinci), both of whom were subjects of paintings completed by Warhol in the early 1960s. While these faces have a traceable history in Warhol's oeuvre, they were resurrected by the artist nearly twenty years later in a quite startling way. Icons of feminine renown, dwelling in the world of museum and movie goddesses, the faces are now expanded to mural dimensions. But the decorative potential of these repetitive images is undermined by the pervasively haunting quality of memory, in part because of the artist's re-creation of the image as a photographic negative that reverses our sense of solid and void, flesh and spirit. The colors also effect this sense of a ghostly emanation. These relics of secular divinities function as a register of both public memory and the memory of the artist himself as he looks back on his own career. It is a mood of retrospection that characterizes Warhol's late work, which includes moody self-portraits, a series devoted to skulls, and an installation of dramatic shadow paintings.
—SRGM

Tom Wesselmann

b. 1931

Tom Wesselmann was born February 23, 1931, in Cincinnati, Ohio. As a youth, he did not intend to pursue a career in the arts. He completed his undergraduate studies at the University of Cincinnati and received a degree in psychology. Wesselmann's college career was briefly interrupted when he was drafted into the United States Army and sent to Fort Riley, Kansas, to study aerial photography for strategic interpretation. It was during his military service that he started drawing, creating humorous cartoons. In 1954 he began taking classes at the Art Academy of Cincinnati; two years later he moved to New York and enrolled at Cooper Union to pursue his artistic interests. Wesselmann would soon become friends with Jim Dine and Claes Oldenburg, influential artists who introduced him to the New York avant-garde of the time.

While attending summer school in 1959, Wesselmann began making collages. Attaching bits of quotidian detritus to modestly sized pieces of composition board, he created schematic interiors with figures and still lifes. Wesselmann enjoyed the seductive qualities of commercial goods, and gradually he moved away from abstraction toward materials and images culled from advertising and consumer culture. His paintings of the early 1960s include familiar products and brand-name foods like Coca-Cola and Lipton Tea, as well as reproductions of works by other artists like Henri Matisse and Piet Mondrian, among fruits and other more traditional still-life subjects. Sometimes Wesselmann would attach actual objects to his two-dimensional surfaces in order to achieve an added realism; for example, a work from 1962 depicting a kitchen employs a glowing fluorescent light that can be turned on and off, a real faucet, and a cupboard that opens to reveal soap pads and other household goods.

Wesselmann would frequently include a female nude in his still lifes, and in 1961 he began to pursue the theme with some intensity. Enamored of, but also frustrated by, Willem de Kooning's seminal series of *Women* paintings (1950–55), Wesselmann quickly sensed that figuration had gone as far as the prevailing artistic tendencies would permit. Distancing himself from Abstract Expressionism, Wesselmann set out to develop an artistic lexicon of his own in his famous *Great American Nude* series. Several of these were included in his first solo exhibition at New York's Tanager Gallery, organized by artist Alex Katz in 1961.

In 1962 Wesselmann was included in the *International Exhibition of the New Realists* at the Sidney Janis Gallery in New York, a prophetic survey of early Pop art from Europe and the United States. He went on to have solo shows in New York at the Green Gallery in 1962–65, and at Sidney Janis, where he would exhibit his work into the 1990s.

In the early 1980s Wesselmann's aesthetic took on a more reductive quality, and he began using laser technology to make simplified steel and aluminum cutouts of his nudes and still lifes. From his early collages to these more recent pieces, the objects are always rendered within a tangible, pictorial space that refers back to traditional still-life, landscape, and figurative painting. Wesselmann's art has been the subject of numerous retrospectives in galleries and museums throughout Europe, Japan, and the United States. He maintains a studio in New York.

PLATE 29
Still Life #45, 1962
Oil, printed reproductions, and plastic relief
on canvas
35 x 48 inches
Sonnabend Collection

Tom Wesselmann's *Still Life #45*, a mixed-medium work from 1962, first strikes the viewer with a powerfully iconic image, then gradually reveals shades of complex artistic experimentation. A glistening, roasted turkey is placed front and center, taking up almost the entire picture plane. It is set against a polychrome background composed of four Kodachrome hues—red, orange, yellow, and blue—painted in broad, horizontal stripes across the entire width of the canvas. From the work's left edge peek three cutout roses, painted on a piece of board with the freehand loops of a practiced commercial style. The use of a collage technique in Wesselmann's work is unmistakable. The turkey—a vacuum-formed plastic supermarket display—projects forcefully into the viewer's space, while the roses create actual shadows on the picture's surface. The initial effect resembles that of a photographer's preparatory staging—a dress rehearsal for a "real" painting, complete with color chart and proxy bouquet. But the lasting impression is of an artist profoundly invested in the formal issues of painting: composition, figure-ground relationships, and color.

Wesselmann's two best-known groups of work—the *Still Life* series, from 1962–64, and the *Great American Nude* series, begun in 1961—betray the idiosyncratic approach underlying his fascination with painting. His use of instantly recognizable subject matter and his cool pseudo-realist visual style link

Wesselmann to such Pop artists as Roy Lichtenstein and James Rosenquist. In fact, Wesselmann's work is also profoundly indebted to the painterly innovations of Abstract Expressionists like Willem de Kooning, an artist he particularly admired. Wesselmann's *Still Life #45*, for example, with its strong central motif balanced against an allover ground, echoes, with a decade's ironic distance, de Kooning's mid-1950s *Women* series.—RH

PLATE 30

Still Life #21, 1962
Acrylic and printed reproductions on board,
with concealed tape recorder
48 x 60 inches
Private collection

In the early 1960s artists began to approach
the canvas not just as a flat surface to be
painted, but as something potentially
sculptural by adding three-dimensional
elements to the two-dimensional surface.
For example, Robert Rauschenberg sometimes
included working mechanical devices in his
Combines, bringing the assemblage technique
into the realm of functional capability;
embedded in one such work, *Broadcast*
(1959), is a homemade sound system,
complete with adjustable knobs, that emits
the white noise of radio static. It may have
been the innovations of Rauschenberg as well
as those of Jasper Johns in the late 1950s
that initially broke new formal and aesthetic
ground, but other artists, including Tom
Wesselmann, pursued such two- and three-
dimensional combinations in their own
manner. Wesselmann's use of appliances
such as telephones, radios, television sets,
and clocks remained faithful to and indeed
further articulated one's expectations of a
product-filled American household despite
his sometimes uncanny juxtaposition of the
pictorial and the three dimensional.

Wesselmann's *Still Life #21* is one of his
more discreet combinations of the mechanical
and the handmade. This tabletop arrangement
of groceries and produce is interrupted by a
human hand dispensing soda into a glass,
a frozen gesture that is underscored by a
soundtrack of the fizzy liquid pouring from the
bottle (a tape recorder playing a continuous
loop of the sound is affixed to the back of the
work). Although the hand pouring the

beverage is that of a man, male figures rarely
make a direct appearance in Wesselmann's
genre scenes. Rather, the masculine presence
is generally understood to be provided by the
viewer/consumer of his works, who functions
as the anticipated character returning after a
long day's work to receive the many pleasures
of home. The implications of such an
exclusively male viewership would become
unavoidable in Wesselmann's ironic and
confrontational *Great American Nude* series
(begun in 1961), in which blatantly erotic
female figures are posed in interiors among
still-life objects.—AM

PLATE 31

Still Life #34, 1963
Acrylic and printed reproductions on panel
47½ inches in diameter
Private collection

Still Life #34 exemplifies Tom Wesselmann's facility at restaging the classical still life as an exploration of convenience and indulgence in American society of the 1960s. He knowingly references and subverts high-art tropes; the tondo-shaped canvas, a form typical in Renaissance portraiture and depictions of religious themes, is here used to frame a seemingly random selection of consumer goods, thus fusing Robert Rauschenberg's proverbial gap between art and life. The typical contents of a seventeenth-century Dutch still life—crystal wine carafe; cornucopia of fruits, nuts, and other delicacies; and freshly-killed game brought in from the hunt—are here updated to a late twentieth-century suburban home; the modern merchant class now imbibes in Coca-Cola, strawberry milk shakes, and an after-dinner cigarette.

Still Life #34 posits itself as a metaphor for a prosperous society that supports the universality of everyday luxuries. The American postwar aesthetic of commercialism and commodification, with its attitude of "more is better," is the vision put forth in Wesselmann's *Still Life* series. As in other pictures from the series, the individual components of *Still Life #34* are rendered in a combination of hand-painted areas and printed reproductions collaged to the surface. The visible brushstrokes that comprise the tabletop, azure vase, and obscure logolike shape evidence the painter's hand, heightening the more linear soda bottle and hyperreal

shells of the Diamond walnuts. The red, blue, and yellow form is an unusual visual code that Wesselmann includes in several other works (e.g., *Still Life #33*, p. 126). Sometimes this oval shape denotes the back of an Art Deco chair that the artist owned and frequently used as a prop, but more often it appears as an abstract, nonspecific logo form free of any corporate or brand name.—AM

PLATE 32

Still Life #33, 1963
Oil and printed reproductions on three
joined canvases
11 x 15 feet
Private collection

After relocating to a more accommodating
studio in 1963, Tom Wesselmann began
working on a larger scale, creating
monumental canvases such as _Still Life #33_.
The source material he used in the early 1960s
gradually evolved from magazine cutouts to
bigger preexisting ads taken directly from
subway stations and window displays, as well
as enormous billboard advertisements. The
billboard aesthetic informs _Still Life #33_,
which despite its grand scale is meant to be
read as a group of objects arranged on a
tabletop. Wesselmann's strategy of grouping
items and products related only by their
consumable nature in a nonhierarchical
arrangement focuses attention on the entire
whole rather than the individual elements of
the work. The shallow foreground practically
subsumes the spectator into the composition.

Still Life #33 might be described as an
exaggerated display of a veritable
workingman's diet. A gleaming portion of
submarine sandwich dominates the frontal
plane, in contrast to its counterparts, which
conform to the strong verticality of the rest of
the composition. The sandwich is cut off at
the edge of the canvas, suggesting that we are
seeing only part of this potentially endless
bounty. Towering behind the sandwich, a
colossal can of Budweiser and a pack of Pall
Mall cigarettes stand firmly if somewhat
ironically as monuments to consumerism.
Nestled between them is the top of an orange,
which echoes the curve of a woman's breast
and may allude to Wesselmann's obsession
with the female nude in other works. The
package of cigarettes is much like the real
advertisements that Wesselmann frequently
attached to his canvases, but this
representation was actually hand painted by
the artist to confound the boundary between
handmade and machine produced. The roses,
which seem to hover overhead, are attached to
the wall, signaling the limits of this interior,
and the right side of the canvas offers a
glimpse of the horizon beyond. Hand-painted
bars of pure color provide firm ground for
the objects, the vertical white and blue
stretching under the still life suggesting the
illusion of depth in the otherwise flat, frontal
composition. The ostentatious scale of the
painting reflects Wesselmann's appetite for
constructing high-keyed domestic landscapes
that surround the viewer with products and
rituals that they know intimately.—AM